RIGHTEOUSNESS
INSIDE
OUT

S T U A R T
C E D R O N E

Pacific Press Publishing Association
Nampa, Idaho
Oshawa, Ontario, Canada

Edited by Kenneth R. Wade
Cover design by Michelle Petz
Typeset in Esprit 11/13.2

The author assumes full responsibility for the accuracy of all facts and quotations cited in this book

Library of Congress Cataloging-in-Publication Data

Cedrone, Stuart, 1952-
    Righteousness inside out : the believer's guide to expe-
riencing the righteousness of Christ / Stuart Cedrone.
        p.   cm.
    Includes bibliographical references.
    ISBN 0-8163-1307-5 (pbk. : alk. paper)
    1. Justification. 2. God—Righteousness. 3. Righteous-
ness. 4. Cedrone, Stuart, 1952- . I. Title.
BT764.2.C43 1996
234'.7—dc20   95-46991
                                                    CIP

96 97 98 99 00 · 5 4 3 2 1

CONTENTS

INTRODUCTION

There was a time in my life when I hit bottom, and although I would never want to go through that ordeal again, I can see now that it turned out to be a blessing, for our heavenly Father used that period to teach me lessons that I doubt I could have learned in any other way. The most important thing I learned was how to accept the almost unbelievable grace that God has bestowed upon us in Christ. When one is at the very bottom, he (or she)* has nothing to offer to the Almighty; thus, he becomes convinced that unless our great God has accomplished everything for his total healing and restoration, then he is surely lost.

I spent approximately two years believing that I *was* surely lost, for I was certainly in what seemed a hopeless condition of deep depression and total bondage. But God was able to break through an almost impregnable wall of pride and unbelief, and, in so doing, He revealed to me the marvelous extent of His grace. I have asked that He never allow me to forget what He has done for me, for I want it always to be fresh and alive in my heart and mind.

In the following pages I will explain exactly how I believe the Lord attempts to draw each of us into a deep and fulfilling fellowship with Himself that invariably lifts an individual into His joy. And please remember that I am speaking as one who was at the very bottom, as one who thought that things like victory and power and peace and joy and upliftment were hopelessly beyond his grasp. Now if the Lord drew *me* into a joyous and victorious fellowship with Himself, then I know He can do the same for you.

Trust the Lord to fulfill your deepest longings for a blessed life of purity and fulfillment, for He is surely able to satisfy this desire of your heart "exceedingly abundantly above all that you ask or think."

· PRAISE THE LORD ·

---

*In this book, I want to address individuals, not groups. I find it awkward to write "he or she" constantly, so in consultation with my editor, I have chosen to regularly indicate that I am writing to both men and women by placing "(or she)" in parentheses at the beginning of a paragraph but then to finish out the paragraph writing "he." I hope that no one will take offense or feel slighted by this attempt to avoid awkward constructions.

6

CHAPTER 1

JESUS·DID·IT·ALL

There is much I could write about personal aspects of my life, but I wonder how relevant that would be. I must tell you a little about myself, though, so you can understand that what I write comes from my own experience of searching for righteousness and salvation.

I came to an awareness of my need of salvation in the mid-seventies through a Bible seminar that focused on the prophecies in the books of Daniel and Revelation. I had just graduated from college, and I was looking for answers to the many questions that I had about life. I responded enthusiastically to the Bible truth that I learned, and I believe I was sincere in my devotion to the Lord at that time. I had a reasonable understanding of the centrality of Christ to one's personal salvation, but I certainly did not begin to realize the completeness of His victory in my behalf. I struggled with various temptations (principally those of appetite), and I can see now that I never fully understood the victorious and fulfilling path of the gospel (although I could certainly talk a good talk on righteousness by faith). I fell out of church fellowship after a few years, and I felt very self-righteous in doing so, for I also did not understand either the importance or the method of working within the body of Christ. I continued to cling to the forms of religion, but, without realizing it, I was growing colder and deader inside. In any event, when I hit bottom, I suddenly saw everything in my life in a different light. It was as if a set of blinders had been stripped from my eyes. I saw the arrogance, the pride, the cowardice, and the hypocrisy. I wanted to die—literally. I was certain there was no hope for me to be in the Lord's kingdom, and since I had never experienced any sort of spiritual fullness in the Christian walk, I honestly wondered why I hadn't lived my life as a "worldling" so that I could have at least enjoyed some release before being burned in the lake of fire.

I cannot begin to express the anguish, the depression, the humiliation, and the despair that I experienced at that time. Truly, there was nothing but deadness and pollution in my soul. My whole head was sick and my whole heart faint. I can honestly say before God that I would not wish that experience on my worst enemy, for it is like death itself.

Now one thing that characterized my life at that time (besides depression, remorse, and despair) was bondage. I was an individual who was completely enslaved by sin (principally that of indulgence), and I saw no escape. The problem was this: I had always been one who thought of salvation in the following terms: "Whatever it takes to get me to Your Kingdom, Lord, You'll have to do it." In other words, I would think along the lines of, "Whatever trials are necessary, Lord. Whatever chastening. Whatever rebukes"—and on and on. Of course, I had always thought of myself as someone who could bear up under this crushing load that was necessary for deliverance. When I hit bottom, however, I knew that I could not bear up under anything. What was I then to do? Death seemed to be the only viable alternative.

What I did not understand at this time is that our salvation is effected by a lifting up, not a beating down. In other words, the key to continual victory in the Christian walk is, I believe, *transcendence*, not submission. Now, it is certainly true that we must submit to the Lord, but what I formerly failed to understand is that this experience is fully ours in Christ, for it was He who was beaten into submission (Isaiah 53:5). It was He who was made perfect through suffering (Hebrews 2:10).

It was He who bore the chastisement that is needful for our peace (Isaiah 53:5). I had failed to see that this was an aspect of my salvation that I needed to claim by living faith. I was in need of acknowledging that all of this whatever-it-takes type of suffering and discipline is *already accomplished* in Christ, and, further, that it is *fully mine* in Him. I have since come to believe that all that God asks of me is that I set my heart and mind—not toward being braced for trial and suffering—but rather toward simply abiding in the One who has *already borne* all of this in my behalf. When I do simply this, I experience only the *fruit* of this suffering, which is the transcendence of our glorified Saviour.

To summarize an important lesson that I learned, then: it was our Lord Jesus who submitted to "whatever it took." It was He who endured to the end (Matthew 24:13). And because of His victory, the Father has raised Him in living power to His right hand in a glorified body that is fully beyond the consequences of sin.[1] And, miracle of miracles, all of this is mine (it is *mine*) by faith. And, of course, it is yours by faith too.

Now allow me to ask: Do you agree with what I have written in the previous two paragraphs? If you do not, then I hope you will bring this issue before the Lord in prayer. I do not advise this in a self-righteous manner. That is, I am not saying to you, "Hey, I've got the truth here; pray about it until you see matters as I do." On the contrary, I continue to pray fervently about this matter myself. Nevertheless, I feel driven to emphasize what I believe to be the completeness of Christ's victory in our behalf simply because I had reached a point in my own experience where I knew that I had absolutely *nothing* to give toward my salvation. I knew that I could acknowledge truth, and I knew that I could cry out for deliverance in Christ, but I also knew that this was *all* I could do. I thus concluded that since the Lord stated in His Word that my salvation is fully accomplished in Christ, and since He also stated that all I had to do was to take Him at His Word in this area, then whenever I came to something in my Christian walk that seemed to necessitate that I *do* something, well, I was going to ask the Lord to reveal to me how this aspect of my salvation was accomplished in Christ. I believe that He has done this every step of the way. In other words, whenever I have come to a point in my experience where I have felt unable to meet the conditions that seem to be set forth for salvation, I have asked the Lord to reveal to me their completion in Christ, and I believe He has done this. And every step has been a lifting up, not a beating down. Furthermore, every step has resulted in greater consecration to His will and thus greater joy in Christ.

So, another important lesson that I learned from my state of absolute hopelessness and helplessness is this: if I am struggling with something I feel incapable of managing, then I simply ask the Lord to reveal to me how this is accomplished *for me* in Christ. He has never failed to do this.

One final point that I should mention is this: when I had hit bottom, I knew that I could not do anything for the Lord, not merely because I had no strength to do it, but also because I had no character. In other words, I had reached the point where I had to say to the Almighty, "You know what You're dealing with, Lord. I am nothing but evil through and through. From the top of my head even to the soles of my feet, there is no soundness in me. My whole head is sick, and my whole heart faint. If You leave me for a *moment*, then the *BIG ME*— the selfish, uncaring, I-don't-care-about-anything-or-anyone person who inhabits this flesh—is going to dive face first into some sinful indulgence."

Now I realize that, at this point, one might come in with the "whatever it takes" line. That is, one might say something like, "I'm evil through and through, Lord, so whatever it takes to get me to Your kingdom, well, You'll have to do it. I put it in Your hands in Jesus' name. Amen."

What you must understand, however, is this: For me it

wasn't a matter of "whatever it takes" because I knew what the Lord was dealing with, and what He was dealing with was someone who was *incorrigible*, someone who would *never* learn. Beat me. Chasten me. Rebuke me—no matter. I just flat out wasn't going to change (Job 34:31, 32, RSV). When the "pull" of the evil one was upon me, I was *always* one to dive in. I could resist anything but temptation.

For me there was no issue of "whatever it takes" because I knew that *nothing* would make any difference. I could not be enlightened into resisting. I could not be chastened into resisting. What then could I do? I simply did the one thing that I was *capable* of doing: I laid it all upon the Lord. (I mean I laid it all upon Him.) And guess what? I found that the Lord *really did* accomplish my salvation—fully and completely—in Christ.

Once again, the reason why I believe the whatever-it-takes prayer is not appropriate is because the Lord has *already* done whatever it takes. He has no need to do to you or to me that which He has already done to His Son—for example, make Him perfect (in submission) through suffering (Hebrews 2:10). Do you see this? I believe it is a most important point. All you and I need to do is merely to claim as our own what Christ *alone* has earned and what Christ *alone* deserves. The Lord *desires* that we do this, for He has told us over and over again in His Word that He "so loved the world" that He gave His only begotten Son for its redemption. We must look away from ourselves (which is where all of this whatever-it-takes type of thinking leads us), and focus instead on our living Saviour. Once again, *He* is the One who submitted to "whatever it took." And because He has done this, the Father has raised Him from the dead in living power and exalted Him to His right hand in a glorified body that is *fully beyond* the consequences of sin. As I stated before, all of this is ours (it is *ours*) by faith. (Amazing—almost unbelievable—but true.)

Now, going back to my own experience, when I began to understand these things, I likewise began to understand that my salvation *really was* accomplished in Christ. I was forced to acknowledge that I had not yet claimed this salvation as my own through faith; nevertheless, I had at least come to know that it was there for the asking. I had also begun to realize that this salvation truly was a *gift* (praise the Lord!)—something that must simply be received.

Please understand that I did not think I *deserved* this gift of salvation. I did not think I *deserved* to be ushered into the favor of God and to be treated as His Son. This was the heart of the battle, really. For I knew all too well that I was a sinner who would never learn; thus, I likewise knew that what I deserved was death. But if the Bible really is the Word of the Lord, then I was compelled to acknowledge that it wasn't His will that I die. It wasn't His will that I wallow in sin. Miracle of miracles, our pure and holy God knew exactly what He was dealing with, and yet He *still* affirmed that He desired my salvation. Furthermore, He affirmed that He had fully accomplished this in Christ, and that all I had to do was to take Him at His Word (claim this salvation by faith). So, because of this, I decided to claim certain promises of God that would allow me to live in an expectant mode, where I was always and everywhere anticipating some blessing from Him as a fruit of my salvation. (This replaced the "dreading" mode where I was always and everywhere anticipating some chastisement or rebuke.) The two promises that I chose were Psalm 23:6 and Psalm 62:5. They are both very simple promises, but this is precisely what I needed at this time—simplicity. Here they are:

> ***Surely goodness and mercy***
> ***shall follow me all the days of my life.***
> ***(Psalm 23:6)***

> ***My soul, wait thou only upon God;***
> ***for my expectation is from him.***
> ***(Psalm 62:5)***

Again, I claimed these promises by faith in the finished

work of Christ.[2] I knew that I didn't deserve any "goodness and mercy" from the Lord, and I also knew that I didn't deserve to be "expecting" anything from Him; nevertheless, I *was* certain that the *Lord Jesus* deserved these things. Thus, I claimed all of this in His name.

The Lord quickly blessed me by showing that the way to be lifted up into His salvation was to be reaching out to others. (It took such a long time to have a living experience in this—I am so selfish!) I would be in a situation, for example, where I might be battling some impending temptation to sinful indulgence, and then an opportunity would arise to reach out and help someone, and—presto!—the temptation would be gone (*gone!*). I was lifted above it (*far* above it!). I thus claimed Ephesians 2:8-10 where the Lord promises that He has a path of good works laid out beforehand for each one of us. I needed the assurance that there would always be some act of benevolence that the Lord had waiting for me that would lift me above the clamorings of my incorrigible flesh. This promise gave me that assurance.

I then claimed Psalm 119:37:

> ***Turn away mine eyes from beholding vanity;***
> ***and quicken thou me in thy way.***

I needed this promise because I needed the assurance—not only that the Lord had a path of good works for me, but also the assurance that He would *quicken* me in this path so that I would (1) discern it and (2) walk in it. Again, I claimed all of this by faith in the Lord Jesus (because I knew that everything was accomplished in Him and because I also knew that the Lord had given Him to me fully).

Now if you do this, then I believe you will begin to see the Lord work in your life. Two things the Lord did (almost immediately) for me were these: He brought children into my life in the form of two young girls that a sister from the local church was caring for as a foster parent. What a blessing! I will not elaborate on all the details of this experience, but I think that most people know what a joy it is to be around children whom the Lord has brought into your life and to try (in His might) to bring them up in His path. It is such a great means of being lifted beyond oneself. The Lord also opened the way for me to become involved in a local prison ministry of our church. Again, what a blessing! What great strength and joy one receives when he or she is actively witnessing for the Lord and leading other needy individuals into fellowship with Him!

Now I hope that these experiences will help you to see, not only how the Lord lifts us above our incorrigible flesh, but also how—from the world's perspective—this very lifting up is perceived as "submission to the Lord"! In other words, looking after the children and reaching out to the prisoners were, from *my* perspective, simply an answer to prayer. The Lord had graciously entrusted me with two fulfilling activities that He knew would lift me up in Him. Individuals who did not know the Lord or His saving power interpreted matters as follows: "Boy, Stu is doing all of this other stuff, and now he's babysitting for children and doing prison ministry as well." The world perceived that I was doing those things as a means of submitting to the Lord, but the reality was that this submission was fully accomplished in Christ, and I was merely allowing myself to be lifted up in Him. In short, I was merely partaking of the *fruit* of this submission (His submission), even the victorious life of a risen Christ. Praise the Lord.

So, to repeat one last time (I honestly do not think this point can be overemphasized): I do not believe we should think in terms of the Lord having to accomplish anything in *us* for our salvation. Now I do not deny, of course, that the Lord *does* have to accomplish something in us. My point is merely that I do not believe that we should think in these terms, for I believe that thinking in these terms effectively prevents the work from being accomplished. There is a process of sanctification, to be sure, that must take place in each of our lives, but sanctification, like justification, is by faith alone. That is, it is accomplished by taking the Lord at His Word. I will develop this theme more fully in subsequent chapters, but the key point to remember at this juncture, I believe, is this: whenever we discern something that needs to be accomplished for our salvation, we are to look to the perfect life of our Saviour and say, "*He* did it, Lord, and by Your grace I claim His reward as my own." That's right—we claim the reward of a perfect life of obedience and submission even while despairing of ever being able to live such a life ourselves. This, I believe, is the true meaning and substance of grace. It is claiming the reward and the deservedness of Someone else—even that of our Lord Jesus. I further believe that this is the only way we become capable of being truly obedient ourselves. In other words, I believe it is only when our proud, self-righteous hearts are fully broken by the mercy and grace of God that we are finally brought to the point where we *are* able to walk, even as He walked.

I feel compelled to state once again that each of us must come to Christ and claim His fullness as our own, even while we are polluted sinners who feel hopelessly bound by sin. Our Saviour *desires* that we do this, for He says,

> ***Come unto me, all ye that labour***
> ***and are heavy laden.***
> ***(Matthew 11:28)***

And, again, He says,

> ***Him that cometh to me I will in no wise cast out.***
> ***(John 6:37)***

Taking our Lord at His Word in this area and thus claiming all of His fullness as my own was the only means that allowed me to be delivered from my hopelessness, my bondage, and my utter, utter despair.

I will close this chapter by telling you how all of this presents itself to my mind. It is as if Someone denied Himself for

His entire life so that He could cultivate the character and the discipline to be a fit ruler of a kingdom. I, on the other hand, spent my days indulging myself—even though I knew it was selfish and wrong. I was just too self-centered to care about anyone but myself. When the day of reckoning arrived and I was filled with remorse for having squandered so many years, the Person who deserved all of the goodness and blessing asked the King of the universe if all of His deservedness and merit could be given to me. The King then said, "According to his faith, be it done unto him."

You may say, "But I have no faith!" I'll save that discussion for a later chapter. For now, I simply want to emphasize once again that I believe it is of the utmost importance that each of us steadfastly refuse to let any focus come upon ourselves. Instead, we must keep claiming before the Father the deservedness of the Lord Jesus. The Father *desires* that we do this, for He knows that it is our only hope for deliverance.

> *Thanks be to God, Who gives us the victory*
> *through our Lord Jesus Christ.*
> *(1 Corinthians 15:57, RSV)*

· P R A I S E T H E L O R D ·

---

1. My thought on this topic was clarified by Andrew Murray's wonderful little devotional classic, *Abide in Christ* (Springdale, Penn.: Whitaker House, 1979), 70.

2. When I use the phrase "the finished work of Christ," I am referring simply to His life of perfect obedience that was lived on this earth in our behalf. I also recognize that Christ has an ongoing work of high-priestly ministration in the heavenly sanctuary and that the work of atonement was thus not completed on Calvary.

CHAPTER 2

THE·NEW·BIRTH

I believe there is no topic of greater importance than that of the new birth. I would even go so far as to say that I do not believe that anything in this book will help you in the least if you are not—at some point—born again, for our first birth is unto death; thus, it is only the second, or new birth, that leads to life eternal.

John 3 explains the importance and the centrality of the new birth. In this chapter our Lord states that "Except a man be born again, he cannot see the kingdom of God" (verse 3). This statement leaves no room for compromise or ambiguity.

The aspect of the new birth that I want to deal with in chapters two and three is experiential reality. That is, the effect of the new birth in the life of the believer is that he or she has a very definite *experience* with God. It is this experience with God that forms the spiritual foundation of the life of faith.

Before I proceed, I should acknowledge that one must always test his or her experience by the clear statements of Scripture. The gospel message of salvation is an *objective* message that is not dependent upon anything that occurs in the interior life of the believer. That is, the gospel message of salvation is a message about the historical facts of Christ's life, death, and resurrection in our behalf (see 1 Corinthians 15:1-4); thus, one's hope for forgiveness and eternal life is grounded in Christ rather than in any personal religious experience. The fact remains, however, that the Lord has redeemed us in Christ so that we may have fellowship with Him, and until we have a firsthand, conscious experience of this fellowship, we are separated and alienated from the source of our life and hope. We still have all of our theoretical knowledge, and we still have all of our devotional practices, but apart from a definite *experience* with the Almighty through Christ, these avail us nothing. They are but empty religious forms that are utterly devoid of the life and substance of personal salvation.

We must be born into the fellowship of the Father and the Son (see 1 John 1:3). We must taste and see that the Lord is good (see Psalm 34:8). We must drink of that water that will become in us a well of water springing up into everlasting life (see John 4:14). *This* is our need.

Do you have a definite experience in these things? If you do not, then I believe your condition is serious indeed, and I further believe that the Lord desires—above all else—to bring you to the point in your experience where you are able to confidently say, "By God's grace I have been born again. I have been mercifully ushered into the Land of Promise, and I now enjoy fellowship with the Father and the Son."

 The new birth is God's work; it is not your work. You must realize also that—as with *all* of the Lord's work in the life of the believer—it is a work that is to be received by faith.

Let me share with you my own experience in this area as I think it will show clearly the way of failure as well as the way of success.

There was a time, not too long ago, when I was dead in trespasses and sins. This death pervaded every aspect of my being, and it seemed to me as if there were no spiritual life in me, for I had no desire to pursue the things of God, and I felt nothing but languor, depression, and despair.

Do you know what I did? For months and months I pleaded with God to give me a new heart. I pleaded with God to put His Spirit within me. In short, I pleaded for the new birth. And do you know what it got me? Nothing. I was still dead inside after all those months of pleading.

Finally, as I was about to give up in despair, the Lord mercifully broke through to my darkened mind. I remember that my thought process at the time was something like this: *Wait a minute! The Lord has promised to give me a new heart! I have His Word on this! I do not have to plead for something that He has promised to give! I have only to claim it in Christ!* From that moment on I did just that—and everything changed.

The well-known promise that I claimed was Ezekiel 36:26, 27:

> *A new heart also will I give you,*
> *and a new spirit will I put within you:*
> *and I will take away the stony heart out of your flesh,*
> *and I will give you an heart of flesh.*
> *And I will put my spirit within you,*
> *And cause you to walk in my statutes,*
> *and ye shall keep my judgments, and do them.*

From that time forward, I no longer pleaded with God about this matter. I simply claimed His promise in the name of Christ. Despite my deadness to spiritual things, I took a statement from the Bible, and I presented it to the Almighty in the name of His Son. That's all I did.

I believe that the most important part of my claiming the promise at that time was this: the Lord had put it in my heart to make a *demand* upon Him (in the name of Christ, of course), and then to expect to *receive* what I had demanded because He had promised to *give* it. In short, the Lord had put it in my heart to *hold Him to His Word.*

About a day or two after having done this, I was at work and something happened, and I sprang forward to assist someone. I remember thinking, *That wasn't me!* because I was all too aware at this time that I was so dead that I did not have even the *physical energy* to do such a thing, let alone the spiritual inclination. My action revealed to me that the Lord was beginning to work in me "to will and to do of his good pleasure" (Philippians 2:13). I realized that He had given me a new heart that was responsive to His promptings—one in which He *lived*.

The reason I knew that the Lord was working in me at this time was not that I suddenly felt transformed into a loving and compassionate person, for I can assure you that I did not feel this way at all. On the contrary, I still felt dead and hardened and sinful, and I was most assuredly in need of much growth before I would begin to experience any sort of spiritual fullness in Christ. But it was *because* I still felt hardened and sinful that I knew it was the Lord's working in me that had resulted in this act of benevolence, for there was surely nothing in my own sinful heart that could have produced it.

I think you will find that the Lord will attempt to work in your life also in such a way that the quickening power of the Holy Spirit will cause you to respond spontaneously to human need. Oswald Chambers, author of the well-known devotional classic *My Utmost for His Highest*, explains love in this way: "The characteristic of love is spontaneity." He goes on to say that "When His Spirit is having His way with us, we live according to His standard without knowing it, and looking on back we are amazed at the disinterestedness of a particular emotion, which is the evidence that the spontaneity of real love was there." Chambers' rationale for making these statements is the following: "The springs of love are in God, not in us."[1] I believe this perspective is in complete accord with Scripture.

Take, for example, the statement that our Lord made to Nicodemus concerning the new birth: "The wind blows where it wills, and you hear the sound of it, but you do not know whence it comes or whither it goes; so it is with every one who is born of the Spirit" (John 3:8, RSV). Also, consider His statement to the Samaritan woman: "The water that I shall give him shall be in him a well of water springing up into everlasting life" (John 4:14). Imagine a kite soaring in the sky or a raft rushing along a mighty stream. A kite soars in the sky because of the motion of the wind, right? Likewise, a raft rushes down a stream because of its buoyancy and the movement of the water. Now, if the motion of the wind and water represent the power of the Holy Spirit in our lives, then each of us should *experience* His movement in our hearts. That is, each of us should have a spiritual experience of life and buoyancy as the Holy Spirit moves upon us. The Holy Spirit is a Person of the Godhead whose presence must be a *reality* in our lives. When His presence *is* a reality in our lives, then all of our works in the life of faith will flow from *His* life, not ours. Acts of mercy and caring will then spring forth spontaneously from His fully benevolent nature.

Of course, not all experiences in the Lord are identical nor are the ways that we are ushered *into* these experiences identical. The Lord knows the best way to reach a person and to keep him or her secure in personal fellowship with Himself. The Lord has used a certain way to reach me. He may use a very different way to reach you, and you may have a somewhat different experience in the Lord.

Nonetheless, I believe there are aspects of the born-again experience that are common to all. These common aspects are enumerated by the apostle Paul in his epistle to the Galatians (see Galatians 5:22, 23). If I were to compile a list of essential elements, I would emphasize the sense of peace and upliftment that the Lord gives to us. Indeed, the first recorded words of our resurrected Lord to His gathered disciples were "Peace be unto you" (Luke 24:36; John 20:19), and I believe it is this glorious sense of peace in the believer's heart that confirms that the Lord is truly in control of his or her life and that he or she may safely rest in His love. It is also this sense of peace that undergirds all the works of faith that ensue in the life of the believer.

Can you identify with this? Are you able to confidently assert that you have this sort of experience with the Almighty? Have you felt the glorious sense of His peace breathed into your soul? Have you felt it drive out all of the care and perplexity of life? Have you felt this sense of peace come alive with the force of His quickening power?

Returning to the account of my own deliverance: after I had sprung forward to assist the individual, I felt a twinge of thankfulness, and I thanked the Lord for His mercy and grace toward me.

Thankfulness is important, for through it the Holy Spirit is able to penetrate more deeply into your sin-hardened heart. This enables Him to motivate you to do even greater works to His glory, which, of course, results in deeper gratitude, which results in still greater works—and on and on. The point is this: once this cycle of recognizing the Lord's work in you and responding to it gets going, it will draw you into a deeper and deeper fellowship with the Father and the Son through the agency of the Holy Spirit.

At the time that I initially recognized this working of the Holy Spirit in me, I was dead, dead, dead. I was not enjoying any deep fellowship with the Lord. Nevertheless, the Lord had put it into my heart to hold Him to His Word (and He will do this for you); thus, even in the midst of my depression and despair, I could not help but recognize His working in me.

If you feel enshrouded in darkness or despair, simply do the one thing I did. Place the promise that I have mentioned to you (Ezekiel 36:26, 27) before the Lord, and claim it in the name of Christ. I can assure you that if you do but this one thing, the Lord will respond even in the midst of your deadness and despair. Truly, He has given you His Word on this.

I must point out that, although the new birth does indeed usher one into an actual experience with the Almighty, you must not expect to receive any sort of confirmation of your new birth on the level of feeling. The only confirmation that you need is the Word of the Living God—and you *have* that. You must simply accept as true that which you have every *reason* to accept as true (the Word of the Living God). The fact that your sinful heart seems hard does not change in the least what the Almighty has said to you, and what He has said to you is this: "I will take out the stony heart and give you a new one." If you will but cling to this promise unflinchingly in the midst of sin and darkness and despair, then the Lord will proceed to usher you into a rich experience with Him, and you will soon sense His fellowship and acceptance.

If you are at a point in your experience where you believe that you are simply unable to lay hold of any promise by faith, then simply confess this unbelief to the Lord. That is something you *can* do—so do it. Just confess it, and cry out for deliverance. The Lord will meet you right where you are (as He always does), and He will begin to strengthen your faith to claim all of His fullness.

He did it for me. I know He can do it for you. Trust Him!

This is life eternal,
that they might know thee, the only true God,
and Jesus Christ, whom thou hast sent.
(John 17:3)

· P R A I S E   T H E   L O R D ·

---

1. Oswald Chambers, *My Utmost for His Highest* (Westwood, New Jersey: Barbour & Co., 1963), p.121.

CHAPTER 3
THE·EFFECTS·OF THE·NEW·BIRTH

Because the new birth is so central to one's salvation in Christ, I would like to address a few matters in this chapter that will show how absolutely vital this experience is to all that occurs in the life of faith.

First of all, please note that the Scriptures state the following:

> *The first man Adam was made a living soul;*
> *the last Adam was made a quickening spirit.*
> *(1 Corinthians 15:45)*

Now this "last Adam" is, of course, our Lord Jesus, and the important point that I believe we must all understand is this: When an individual is born again by the grace of God in Christ, Jesus begins to live in him *as* this quickening Spirit, and it is this very quickening that forms the spiritual basis of everything that occurs in the life of faith. Indeed, I would even go so far as to assert that nothing in the Christian walk has any true substance or meaning apart from this, for even the Bible itself is but a dead book apart from the life-giving power of our Lord, and those who read it without a heart that is open to the Spirit's entrance usually become further and further hardened in sin and unbelief.

As I have said, one must always test his or her experience by the clear statements of Scripture, and the gospel message of salvation is an objective message about what God has done in Christ. Therefore, this message is in no way dependent upon anything that occurs in one's interior life.

Having acknowledged that, I will go on to state (strongly!) that when an individual personally accepts by faith the message of salvation as it is in Christ, then he is invariably ushered into an actual *experience* with God. There is simply no way around this. This experience should be characterized by rest and peace, no matter what the external circumstances, and it is likewise one that is filled with the fruit of the Spirit (see Galatians 5:22, 23). Of course, there is normally quite a struggle involved in securing this experience, and one should not be discouraged by this. But this struggle occurs—not because the Lord is unwilling to usher us into His rest and peace—but rather because our proud, sinful hearts are so reluctant to relinquish the control of our lives to the all-knowing and all-merciful One.

In any event, our great need in the church today is not for men and women with more knowledge or more ability or more "willpower." Rather, our great need is for men and women who have allowed themselves to be ushered into the rest and peace of the Lord. Our great need is for men and women who eat the Saviour's flesh, who drink His blood, and who breathe His Spirit.

Now let us consider the more practical aspects of our walk in the Spirit. Take, first of all, the all-important matter of our loving one another as Christ has loved us so that our lights can shine before men and thus bring glory and honor to God. Clearly, this is an area of our lives that is of the utmost importance, for, above all else, our Saviour has called each of us to a life of heartfelt service to others. There is simply no way anyone can fulfill this ministry of servanthood apart from a genuine experience with the Lord and His quickening power, for apart from this, all our actions are polluted with selfishness, vanity, and pride. When, however, one is truly born again, acts of mercy and benevolence become spontaneous, inspired by the life-giving power of Jesus.

If you are not experiencing the quickening power of our Lord, then it is impossible for acts of heartfelt service to spring forth spontaneously from His life in you. You may be caught in a routine where you are doing things you know a Christian *ought* to do, but that you have no heartfelt *inclination* to do. The problem with this is that this is not a Christian life, for a Christian life is simply a life in which Christ *lives*, and a life in which Christ lives is invariably one that renders *heartfelt* service and obedience. (See Ezekiel 36:25-28; Jeremiah 31:33; Hebrews 8:10; Romans 6:17.)

Even if you do feel inclined to help others, if it is not grounded in the Lord's quickening power, then it is grounded in your own human need, and nothing grounded in human need can equate to Christian love because Christian (or agape) love "seeketh not her own" (1 Corinthians 13:5). It cannot, therefore, flow from your own sense of need for the companionship and fellowship of others. It must flow from fullness, not lack; sufficiency, not dependency.

Love is clearly an *other*-regarding impulse. In other words, it is a state of being that is characterized by a desire to seek *another's* welfare—even if it be at the expense of one's own. For this reason, one could justifiably state the principle of love as follows: a doing for the other for the *other's* sake.

Now, if this is what love is, then any act that is motivated by one's own need does not qualify as an act of love. It is actually a selfish act. Clearly, love and my own need are like oil and water: they simply do not mix. Love is an *other*-regarding impulse. It must flow from fullness and not lack. This is why the Bible states that "love is *of* God" (not "of man") and that *He* is love (1 John 4:7, 8). The Bible also states that "our *sufficiency* is of God" (2 Corinthians 3:5).

To summarize, then, acts of genuine benevolence flow only from the quickening power of the Lord, for only the Lord transcends the need and dependency of the human condition. Stated differently, only the high and lofty One is a fully self-fulfilled being (only He has no need of anything beyond His own fullness for completeness and sufficiency); thus, only He can truly do for another for the *other's* sake. For this reason, *we* are able to do for another for his or her sake only as we *share* in the fullness of His uncreated life by the quickening power that He imparts to us in Christ.

Now if you have no firsthand experience of this power, then I urge you to make it your absolute first priority to correct this.

Now just as the Lord's quickening power is central to a life of service in the Lord, so is it also central, I believe, to every other aspect of the life of faith. Take, for example, the area of guidance. We must always, of course, consult the Lord's Word as we seek His guidance in our lives, but for most of the decisions with which we are faced in everyday life, the broad principles of the Bible are too general to provide *specific* direction. Here, again, is where a living fellowship with the Almighty is essential, for I think you will invariably find that if there is any lingering doubt about the Lord's leading after you have sought guidance from His Word and His providential leading, He will dispel this doubt by invigorating you with His quickening power as you take a step of faith in the path that seems most in harmony with His will. Needless to say, if your choice is not in harmony with His leading, then you will recognize this very soon as well because, if you are tuned in to His leading, you soon will sense in your spirit that His life is not there with you.

Of course, our experience with the Almighty must always be tested with the Word of God (1 John 4:1). In other words, one must always examine the fruit of the spirit that is at work in one's life to be certain that it is the fruit of love, joy, peace, patience, kindness, goodness, faithfulness, gentleness and self-control (see Galatians 5:22, 23, RSV). Once this is done, however, and one is assured that the life in him (or her) is indeed in harmony with the life that is depicted in the Word of God, then one must *rely* upon this life to direct him in those situations where specific guidance is needed. One must look to the Almighty and know that

His Spirit will indeed bear witness with one's own spirit and assert that "This is the way walk ye in it" (Isaiah 30:21).

I think you can see the intimate correlation between relying upon God's quickening power for a life of holiness and service and relying upon this same power for guidance, for when we are out of harmony with God's Spirit, we begin to have to force ourselves to do the things of God. Now, I have found that forcing myself to do God's will *always* leads to a time when my "willpower" (if that's what you want to call the power of the flesh) cracks, and I fall into sin. I have thus found that the appropriate response to these times is not to grit my teeth and resolve to gut it out, but rather to bring the matter to the Lord for resolution. He invariably reveals to me what area of my life is in need of readjustment or correction, and, by His grace, I then proceed to confess my waywardness and to cry out for deliverance in Christ. The Lord then proceeds to lift me beyond this obstacle, and His quickening power becomes, once again, the motivating force in my life.

Any Christian who has no living experience with the Almighty through the new birth, will find himself (or herself) doing those things that a Christian is commanded to do but that his or her sinful flesh does not really want to do.

If you are in this state, how can you recognize the Lord's leading in your life? If the way of the Lord seems hard to you, then, like Elijah (when he fled from Jezebel), you must realize that you are running *from* the Lord and His will in your life. Always remember: the ways of the Lord are "ways of pleasantness," and all His paths "are peace" (Proverbs 3:17).

To summarize, then, our life of holiness and service in Christ is intimately related to the Lord's guidance in our lives simply because both are grounded in a living communion with *Him*. When we are standing on the promises of the Word and are thus claiming our true position in Christ, we enjoy a vibrant fellowship with the Father and the Son. Our experience is thus fresh and alive, and the quickening power of the Holy

Spirit energizes our every step to perform the sweet and blessed will of God. We thus recognize that the way of service and holiness (wholeness for God) is the way of the Lord's leading. When, however, this fellowship begins to ebb away and we discern a void in our experience as well as a lack of interest and motivation in the things of God, then this is one of the surest indications that we are not on the Lord's path, and we must immediately bring this matter to the Lord so He can reveal to us the specific nature of our waywardness. We must then confess the sinful ways He reveals to us and proceed to look to Him for forgiveness, healing, and restoration.

I remember when I was in the grip of utter, utter despair, and I saw absolutely no hope for salvation in my life. I was alone in a room, and I was thoroughly convinced that everyone in the world would be better off without me. I saw so clearly how proud and selfish and cowardly and hypocritical I had been all my life. I saw this so clearly that I thought the mere recognition of this fact would kill me—that's how forceful and overwhelming it was. (I honestly remember thinking that someone would come into the room the next morning and find me lifeless on the floor, and I knew that I would *deserve* this end, for I had surely brought all of this crushing shame and remorse upon myself.) Anyway, as I was kneeling there in this polluted and hopeless condition, confessing my wretchedness before the Lord and crying out to Him for deliverance, I remember that His quickening Presence suddenly took hold in my heart, and I was immediately filled with the most blessed sense of forgiveness and acceptance. Truly, I cannot begin to express it. Furthermore, the Lord allowed this flood of grace to continue for hours. I was just kneeling there the whole time, basking in the blessed light of God's mercy and compassion.

That experience blessed me immensely in my Christian growth because it gave substance and legitimacy to my hope of salvation. It provided a foundation of spiritual "realness" that allowed me to move forward in the confident assurance that the

Lord had given me unmistakable evidence of my personal acceptance in Christ. In fact, I remember that the very first thought that I had on the morning following that incident was this: "Whatever happens from here on out, I know there is hope for me."

But, you say, "Our hope should be grounded in the Lord's Word, not our own experience." This is true, of course; nevertheless, when the Lord's Word is so very clear about the actual *experience* of rest and peace that one is ushered into in Christ, well, it is very difficult (even presumptuous, I would say) for one to believe that he has truly laid hold of salvation until this blessed experience of spiritual calm is a *reality* for him.

In any event, regardless of how you feel about this experience, my main point in this chapter is that the quickening of your spirit is the principal means by which the Lord Jesus expresses His life in you. Without this, I honestly do not believe there is any legitimate grounding to your hope of salvation, for, without this, you are as one who is attempting to climb the walls of an infinitely deep well instead of merely allowing yourself to be lifted up by an inexhaustible spring of living water. The bottom line, I believe, is this: The Lord must be *REAL* to you. His very *life* must be something you experience as a supernatural presence in *your* life.

Now if you have no firsthand, conscious experience of the buoyancy and upliftment of the Lord's life, then I would recommend that you cry out to the Almighty for His quickening presence, and I would further recommend that you not relent until you have the blessed assurance that His Spirit has indeed borne witness with your spirit that you are a child of the living God.

By this we know that we abide in him and he in us,
because he has given us of his own Spirit.
(1 John 4:13, RSV)

· P R A I S E   T H E   L O R D ·

CHAPTER 4

SURRENDER

Many Christians believe that our life in the Lord begins with surrender. Virtually all of the individuals with whom I have spoken think of surrender in one of the following ways: "I must surrender to the Lord," or "I must surrender my will to the Lord," or "I must surrender this or that object or inclination to the Lord." However they express it, the end result is the same: Surrender reduces to something that you and I must *do*.

I was once at a point in my life where I could do *nothing*, not even surrender to the Lord. My self-life was too firmly entrenched to admit defeat. The "I" in me was the ruling power, and it seemed that it would rather physically die than allow someone else to take the throne.

Now applying the method that I articulated in chapter one, this is what I did: when I found myself unable to surrender, I simply cried out in my helplessness to the Almighty, and I asked Him to reveal to me how this aspect of my salvation was accomplished in Christ. As I continued to pray and to search the Word of God about this matter, I began to see more and more clearly how foolish I was for once thinking that I or anyone else could surrender to the Lord. I found that surrender—like everything else in the Christian walk—is by faith. That is, it is something that we must claim in Christ.

I believe that until a person reaches the point where he (or she) sees that this aspect of his salvation is fully accomplished in Christ, he will be in a most precarious condition. That is, he will have little, if any, confidence before the Lord to claim the blessings of the Christian walk, simply because he will be ever aware of his lack of total, perfect surrender, and he will thus believe that he has no right to claim anything from the Almighty. There is probably no other area where faith is so severely undermined as right here.

None of the above-mentioned dilemmas will be resolved until one realizes that his or her surrender to the Lord is something that he cannot supply, but rather is something that he must simply claim by faith in Christ. In other words, *Jesus* is the One who lived the life of perfect surrender. All that you or I can do is simply look to that life and then claim it as our own before the Lord.

The objection that someone might offer, of course, is this: "If we cannot even surrender to the Lord, then what *can* we do? Surely there is *something* we contribute to our salvation."

I would say that the only "something" we contribute to our salvation is this: We cry out to the Almighty for deliverance. That's it. That's totally and completely it. Listen to what the Lord's Word says by the prophet Hosea:

32

> ***"They do not cry to me from the heart,***
> ***but they wail upon their beds."***
> ***(Hosea 7:14, RSV)***

This, I believe, is the only real issue in one's salvation—crying out to God from the heart. This is how all of the people who are honest in heart, but who never heard the name of "Jesus" in their lives, will be allowed entrance into the Lord's kingdom. They recognized the need of a higher power, and they cried out to this power, knowing that this was their only hope for deliverance from the pull of sin and death.

Now in case you are thinking that when one makes this the sole condition of salvation, matters are just too easy—well, yes and no. Matters are easy in the sense that there is nothing the Lord requires that we *do* in order to effect our salvation (because all of the "doing" is done in Christ), but they are any-thing *but* easy inasmuch as crying out to the Almighty and admitting that we *cannot* do anything is the absolute hardest thing for proud and arrogant creatures like ourselves to ac-knowledge. We would rather moan and groan and gripe and complain about anything and everything that is wrong in our lives instead of crying out to God from our hearts.

But, if you do resolve to cry out to God and to *trust* Him with your *whole* heart, then you will find yourself engaged in the greatest battle of your life (and you will thus see your need of Christ's victory in this area). You will realize just how *un*-comfortable it is for your proud, self-seeking human nature to place its *complete* trust in a higher power. You would be far more comfortable moaning and complaining about everything that is wrong with your life. All of your elaborate excuses, your gripes and complaints, your possible resentments and hostili-ties—they have become like a nice, soft easy chair or a group of sympathizing friends. You have become accustomed to settling into them. They are comfortable. They keep you protected. They allow you to continue in your own way.

No changes. No disruptions. No discomfort. But, of course, No satisfaction. No fulfillment. No growth.

To cry out to God from the depths of your heart means that you must renounce your right to murmur or to complain to others, for, in crying out to the Almighty, you are enlisting the help of One who, as Sister White says, "is too wise to err and too good to do us harm" (*The Upward Look*, 125). For the unfallen angels, depending on their Creator is the easiest thing to do, but for fallen beings like ourselves, it is the hardest.

When I was struggling with this issue, I asked the Lord to give me a promise from His Word that would help me to rest in the assurance that he had taken the responsibility for my surrender completely upon Himself. Do you know what the promise is that I believe He gave to me? It is one I never would have expected, and it is also one I had never heard used in this context. Here it is:

"Truly, truly, I say to you,
when you were young,
You girded yourself and walked where you would;
but when you are old,
you will stretch out your hands,
and another will gird you
and carry you where you do not wish to go."
(John 21:18, RSV)

Jesus used these words to inform Peter of the type of martyrdom Peter would undergo in order to glorify Him. This type of martyrdom was, of course, crucifixion, and Peter is reputed to have been crucified upside down because he felt too unworthy to be tortured in the same manner as his Lord.

Now in the life of the believer, crucifixion represents the death to self that is indicative of a perfectly surrendered life. So this promise came to represent to me Jesus' assurance that He recognizes my waywardness and that His life in me is sufficient to bring about that which my flesh would never allow; namely, a perfect surrender to my Saviour and Lord.

So, the important point I wish to convey in this chapter is this: Perfect surrender is something that was accomplished in the life of our Lord Jesus Christ, and it is something that God desires that we claim in Him. As in all other areas of the Christian walk, we should not look to ourselves or to our own experiences in this area. Rather, we must steadfastly keep our eyes upon the Lord Jesus and keep claiming His life of perfect submission before the Father. We must always remain in the mode of crying out to God from our hearts. We must admit that we cannot bring ourselves to the point of full surrender, and then, while admitting this state of helpless need, we must claim the perfect submission of the mighty Lord Jesus as our own. We must continue to do this regardless of how bumpy the road seems to be, for this is assuredly the right road, and we can thus rest in the confident assurance that it will lead to total and complete victory in our Saviour.

Praise the Lord for perfect surrender in Christ.

· **PRAISE THE LORD** ·

35

CHAPTER 5
TEMPTATION

Most people don't understand what resisting temptation is all about. They are inclined to think of it in this way: "I must resist it, for God's grace is always sufficient." I would rather say, "You must admit that you *cannot* resist it, and then give it to our Lord, for if your life is identified with His life as it should be, then it is His."

Please allow me to explain.

First of all, you must remember that we are exhorted to pray—not that we enter not into sin—but rather that we enter not into *temptation*. (See Matthew 6:13; Luke 11:4; 22:40, 46.) So it would seem that we must acknowledge at the very outset that it is not the Lord's will that we be battling with worldly or lustful enticements. (I do not say that we never do—only that it is not the Lord's *will* that we do.)

When I was at the very bottom in my experience, I could not resist anything, so I knew that if the Lord were calling me to resist—of all things—*temptation*, then I was surely lost. Furthermore, I had always found that when I had struggled against temptation in the past, I was weakened rather than strengthened by the experience. In other words, even if I came off as "conqueror," I could not help but realize that I always seemed to emerge from such battles somewhat the worse for wear. I would thus say to you the following: It is far better to be spared the battle and by the Spirit's power to live *above* the pull of the wicked one. Remember, God certainly allows us to be placed in various circumstances in order to reveal to us what is in our hearts; nevertheless, He *tempts* no one (see James. 1:13).

Now, to get back to my original point, I believe that the appropriate way to deal with temptation is to admit that we *cannot* resist it and then to give it to the Lord Jesus, for if our lives are identified with His as they should be, then it is surely His. The important point is this: we must all realize that only Jesus has the perfect character and moral integrity to meet the demands of any requirement of salvation. Thus, when it comes to this matter of temptation, we must acknowledge that only He can resist and conquer it (and He has done this—for *us*). Surely the Lord has no desire that we engage in a battle with the evil one that His Son has already won in our behalf.

Consider what our Saviour said to His disciples (to you and to me) as He was about to endure the agony of Gethsemane:

> *Ye are they which have continued*
> *with me in* **my** *temptations.*
> *(Luke 22:28, emphasis supplied)*

I believe that we can apply this to ourselves as well. We, too, are Jesus' disciples, and we can continue with Him in *His* temptations. Now if we will allow the Lord to draw us into a continuous state of watchfulness and prayer (the state that He exhorted His disciples to be in during His temptations [see Luke 22:40, 46]), then I believe that we will never have to bear up under what He has *already* borne up under in our behalf. What would be the point? Remember, our salvation is effected by a lifting up (in Christ), not a beating down (see John 16:33). I believe that continual experiences of temptation, strained submission, agonizing self-sacrifice, and the like are the surest indication that one is resisting—not temptation—but rather God's grace. In other words, it is the stiff-necked person (the one who refuses to be broken) who is continually engaged in endless battles in these areas. He or she is determined to have his or her own way, so his or her will is brought into continual conflict with the will of God. The end result, of course, is unending inner turmoil and temptation. In contrast to this is the one who has sought and claimed full surrender in the Lord. This individual realizes that the ways of the Lord are "ways of pleasantness" and that all His paths "are peace." (Proverbs 3:17). Consider another text:

> *But God, who is rich in mercy, for his great love*
> *wherewith he loved us,*
> *Even when we were dead in sins,*
> *hath quickened us together with Christ,*
> *(by grace ye are saved;)*
> *And hath raised us up together,*
> *and made us sit together in heavenly places*
> *in Christ Jesus.*
> *(Ephesians 2:4-6)*

So, according to this text, God has, of all things, made us sit together in heavenly places in Christ Jesus. (Imagine!) Now, do you think that Christ is ever tempted by some worldly self-indulgence while He is in heaven at the right hand of God? Of course not. Then how can *we* be tempted by such if we are there *in* Him? Clearly, we cannot. The only problem, of course, is that we are there *by faith*, and if our faith does not lay hold of the promise, then, quite simply, we are not there and are thus subject to worldly temptations—as well as to many other things.

As I stated in the initial chapter, the Lord desires that we claim the life of the *risen* Christ who is at His right hand in a glorified body that is *fully beyond* the consequences of sin. *This* is where victory over temptation lies. I hope you will pray and search the Word of God for yourself about this matter in order to see if this is not so. Also, I hope that you will apply this method by living faith to your own experience and see for yourself whether the Lord blesses.

Now one text that individuals often give to me in order to show that the biblical method for dealing with temptation is to *resist* it is the following:

Resist the devil, and he will flee from you.
(James 4:7)

In response to this approach I would say the following: Try it, and see how victorious you are. When push comes to shove in the experience of any sinner like you and me and the heat is really on with regard to a temptation to some long-cherished sin, then the last thing that we will be able to do (or even be *inclined* to do) is to "resist the devil."

Even if you *do* happen to get what you consider to be a victorious resistance, then ask yourself the following question: Do you feel that you could cast your crown at the Saviour's feet at the very moment that you obtained the victory and acknowledge that He *alone* is worthy of glory and honor? Or do you feel that you *yourself* are worthy and superior at such a time. At the very least, I believe that you will find yourself feeling somewhat disdainful of those who do *not* brace themselves to "resist the devil"; thus, your compassionate witness for the Saviour will be greatly undermined.

The key to understanding James 4:7, I believe, is to realize that all of the "doing" with regard to our salvation is done (it is *done*) in Christ. With regard to this specific matter of resisting the devil, do you remember when the mighty Lord Jesus was in the wilderness after having fasted for forty days and forty nights? Do you remember when the devil came and tempted Him? Do you remember what He did? He *resisted* the devil, right? And then what happened? The devil *fled* from Him, right? Well, you claim that victory as yours, because it *is* yours *by faith* (as is every other aspect of our Saviour's life—praise the Lord).

Now, I hope you will personally apply the principle involved in the previous discussion to every biblical passage that seems to be requiring something of you. In other words, if you meet with a passage of Scripture that enjoins that you *do* something, then understand that the Lord is using this text—not in order to motivate you to try to *do* it—but rather to motivate you to see your need of its *fulfillment* in Christ. There is really nothing that you must do when it comes to the matter of your salvation except this: acknowledge the truth and admit that it is not in you to live it. If you merely continue to do this, then you will be driven to cry out for deliverance in Christ, and this deliverance will be supplied. You will thus find that all the necessary "doing" in your life will get done, for as you continue to acknowledge the truth and to cry out for deliverance, the Lord will lead you to grow in the grace and knowledge of our Saviour. You will thus eventually be led to claim the victorious life of the mighty Lord Jesus fully. Praise the Lord.

To summarize, then, the central points of importance in this chapter are these:

1. We should not be living our lives in a constant battle with temptation; if we are, then this is a sign that there is something amiss in our experience with the Lord. We should be living *above* this pull of the wicked one—even in heavenly places in Christ Jesus.

2. If you *do* fall into temptation by being "drawn away of [your] own lust, and enticed" (James 1:14), then the key to victory does not lie in bracing yourself to resist it; rather, the key to victory lies in being *broken* before the Lord during this period and admitting that *any* temptation is too strong for you because you are a born sinner with a heart that loves to stray from Him. You thus *give* the temptation to the Lord and, with a cry that is motivated by your absolute need and helplessness, you demand (yes, *demand*) that He manage it for you.

Always remember that the way to manage temptation is to be, not "braced," but, rather, broken; not strong, but, rather, weak. For when one is broken and weak (in "resistance"), then one is braced and strong (in faith). And faith, of course, is the victory.

· PRAISE THE LORD ·

CHAPTER 6

GROWTH

We are exhorted in the Lord's Word to "grow in grace, and in the knowledge of our Lord and Saviour Jesus Christ" (2 Peter 3:18).

Now, I think we all realize that growth in the Christian life is important, and certainly anyone who takes his life in the Lord seriously should not expect to remain the same babe in Christ as the months and the years pass by. On the contrary, one should expect to see a continually progressing maturity that leads to greater devotion and consecration as one grows in the Lord.

The reality, unfortunately, often appears to be quite opposite. In many cases, individuals become *less*, rather than more, intense in their devotion to the Lord as the years pass by. The fervency and the zeal of the initial conversion experience slowly ebb away, and they become more worldly and accommodating. One cannot help but ask, "Why is this?"

Hannah Smith, a nineteenth-century Quaker woman addressed this issue in her book *The Christian's Secret of a Happy Life*. (I recommend this book to *everyone!*) She affirms that the reason so many Christians do not grow fruitfully in the Lord is that they are not thoroughly planted in the love and favor of God. Since I have found that lack of growth in my own experience is usually traceable to this cause, I would like to elaborate on this point.

First of all, in order to *grow* in grace, one must certainly understand what grace is. The standard definition is "the free, unmerited favor of God." As Hannah Smith points out, however, this definition "expresses only a little of its meaning," for the reality of grace in the life of the believer has a substance and a fullness that "free unmerited favor" fails to capture. Grace in the life of the believer is a realization as well as an experience of "the unhindered, wondrous, boundless love of God, poured out upon us in an infinite variety of ways, without stint or measure, not according to our deserving, but according to His measureless heart of love."[1]

Do you believe this? If you do, then you must grow in *this* if you would grow *at all* in the Christian life. In other words, in order for you to experience the continually progressing maturity of one who is growing in the Lord, you must, as Hannah Smith asserts,

> "be planted in the very heart of this Divine love, be enveloped by it, steeped in it. You must let yourself out to the joy of it, and you must refuse to know anything else. You must grow in the apprehension of it day by day, and you must entrust everything to its care, having not a shadow of doubt that it will surely order all things well."[2]

Again, I must emphasize that if the grace of God is the "unhindered, wondrous, boundless love of God, poured out upon us in an infinite variety of ways" (and it surely is), then you must necessarily grow in *this* if you would grow at all in the Christian life.

Unfortunately, many Christians seem to have no genuine experience of this love of God as it is "poured into our hearts through the Holy Spirit which has been given to us" (Romans 5:5). I fear that this is especially true of many Adventists. We tend to place so much emphasis upon the law of God that it is easy to overlook the fact that the true substance and reality of the Christian life is an *experience* with the Almighty, a *communion* with the Father and the Son through the agency of the Holy Spirit. As the beloved apostle John wrote: "Our fellowship is with the Father and with his Son Jesus Christ" (1 John 1:3).

Now if individuals do *not* have this experience of the love of God poured into his (or her) heart, then it is because, on *some* level, he is embracing a lie rather than the truth. In other words, this individual is refusing to acknowledge his dependency and his need and is choosing rather to cling to his sinful pride and imagined self-sufficiency. For an individual *outside* of the church, the result will be a "worldling" who, for the most part, makes no bones about living a life that is out of harmony with the will of God. For an individual *inside* the church, however, the result will be a legalist who has no true sense of his need of the deservedness of Christ. The practical outcome for this "believer" is that he tries to grow *into* grace instead of *in* it. Hannah Smith writes about such individuals as follows:

> They are like a rosebush planted by a gardener in the hard, stony path with a view to its growing *into* the flowerbed, and which has, of course, dwindled and withered in consequence instead of flourishing and maturing. The children of Israel, wandering in the wilderness, are a perfect picture of this type of growing. They were traveling about for forty years, taking many weary steps, and finding but little rest from their wanderings; and yet, at the end of it all, they were no nearer the promised land than they were at the beginning. . . . All of their wanderings and fightings in the wilderness had not put them in possession of one inch of the promised land. In order to get possession of this land it was necessary first to be in it; and, in order to grow in grace, it is necessary first to be planted in grace. When once in the land of promise, the conquest of the children of Israel was rapid; and when once planted in grace, the growth of the spiritual life be-

comes vigorous and rapid beyond all conceiving. For grace is a most fruitful soil, and the plants that grow therein are plants of a marvelous growth. They are tended by a Divine Husbandman, and are warmed by the Sun of Righteousness, and watered by the dew from Heaven. Surely, it is no wonder that they bring forth fruit "some a hundredfold, some sixty-fold, some thirty-fold."[3]

The one reason why someone seeks to grow *into* the grace of God instead of *in* it, the one reason why someone is content to be planted in a hard, stony path rather than a choice plot of fertile soil, is this: on one level or another he is embracing a lie rather than the truth. He refuses to acknowledge his utter finitude and dependence and chooses rather to believe that he can be like the Most High. As a result, he seeks to deny his deep need of Christ, and he thus falsely imagines himself to be an achiever rather than a receiver.

It should go without saying that no one can live this lie forever; thus, any individual who refuses to acknowledge his need and dependence and thus also refuses to allow himself to be planted in the grace of God will surely become "dwindled and withered in consequence instead of flourishing and maturing."

It should also go without saying that, in this area of growth, the remedy for any deficiency or lack is to be found in the life of our Saviour. People are languishing on the hard, stony path because they have not claimed as their own the deservedness of Christ. Instead, they are looking to themselves for deservedness, and they fail to receive all that God seeks to bestow upon them.

I hope it is clear that the type of growth I have described in this chapter is diametrically opposed to any growth in self-dependence, self-effort, or legality of any kind.

> ***Consider the lilies of the field, how they grow;***
> ***they toil not, neither do they spin.***
> ***(Matthew 6:28)***

And again,

> *"Which of you by taking thought*
> *can add one cubit unto his stature?"*
> *(Matthew 6:27)*

As Hannah Smith rightly concludes: "If our experience is one of toiling and spinning for ourselves great spiritual garments, or one of stretching and straining in our efforts toward spiritual growth, then we can be sure that we are accomplishing nothing.[4]

> *Upon God's will I lay me down*
> *As child upon its mother's breast.*
> *No silken couch, nor softest bed*
> *Could ever give me such sweet rest.*[5]

If there is no experience of the rest depicted in this stanza, then one is not planted in the blessed grace of God and thus is not growing.

It should be emphasized that all growth in grace is a growth in one's realization of how the Lord's favor is *un*merited. In other words, there is a deepening of repentance, a greater sense of helplessness and unworthiness. Christ truly becomes all and in all, and He is seen as one's *only* hope of salvation. An individual who is growing in grace would never think of himself (or herself) as *more* able to keep God's law; rather, he would see the Lord's immutable standard as something that is as far above him as the stars. He does not think of himself as *stronger*; on the contrary, he begins to realize more and more just how utterly weak and helpless he is. Growth in grace is a growth in the *faith* that allows one to claim more and more of the boundless riches that he knows he does *not* deserve. He is able to do this because he finally comes to the point in his life where he sees just how fully Christ deserves them, and he is thus able to claim them confidently in Christ's name because he experiences more and still more of the sweet fellowship with His Saviour that allows him to realize how completely Christ accepts him despite his unworthiness.

Now since growth in the Christian life is a growth in one's realization and experience of the boundless and unhindered love of God, one must be very careful to understand and appreciate fully this love for what it truly is. One must not, for example, allow oneself to believe any of the lies of the devil that would distort and degrade this love into something that it is not. Consider what Hannah Smith says about God's love:

> I sometimes think that a totally different meaning is given to the word "love" when it is associated with God from that which we so well understand in its human application. We seem to consider that Divine love is hard and self-seeking and distant, concerned about its own glory, and indifferent to the fate of others. But if ever human love were tender and self-sacrificing and devoted, if ever it could bear and forbear, if ever it could suffer greatly for its loved one, if ever it were willing to pour itself out in lavish abandonment for the comfort or the pleasure of its objects, then infinitely more is Divine love tender and self-sacrificing and devoted, and glad to bear and to forbear and to suffer, and eager to lavish its best of gifts and blessings upon the objects of its love. Put together all the tenderest love you know of, dear reader, the deepest you have ever felt, and the strongest that has ever been poured out upon you, and heap upon it all the love of all the loving human hearts in the world, and then multiply it by infinity, and you will begin, perhaps, to have some faint glimpses of the love and grace of God.[6]

Now because this area of the love of God is so centrally and vitally important to one's growth in Christ (as well as to every other aspect of one's life of faith and trust in the Saviour), I would like also to include two of my favorite passages from the pen of Ellen White that address it:

All the paternal love which has come down from generation to generation through the channel of human hearts, all the springs of tenderness which have opened in the souls of men, are but as a tiny rill to the boundless ocean when compared with the infinite, exhaustless love of God. Tongue cannot utter it; pen cannot portray it. You may meditate upon it every day of your life; you may search the Scriptures diligently in order to understand it; you may summon every power and capability that God has given you, in the endeavor to comprehend the love and compassion of the heavenly Father; and yet there is an infinity beyond. You may study that love for ages; yet you can never fully comprehend the length and the breadth, the depth and the height, of the love of God in giving His Son to die for the world. Eternity itself can never fully reveal it.[7]

The gift of Christ reveals the Father's heart. It testifies that the thoughts of God toward us are "thoughts of peace and not of evil." Jer. 29:11. It declares that while God's hatred of sin is as strong as death, His love for the sinner is stronger than death. Having undertaken our redemption, He will spare nothing, however dear, which is necessary to the completion of His work. No truth essential to our salvation is withheld, no miracle of mercy is neglected, no divine agency is left unemployed. Favor is heaped upon favor, gift upon gift. The whole treasury of heaven is open to those He seeks to save. Having collected the riches of the universe, and laid open the resources of infinite power, He gives them all into the hands of Christ, and says, All these are for man. Use these gifts to convince him that there is no love greater than Mine in earth or heaven. His greatest happiness will be found in loving Me.[8]

So, can you and I say that we are at least *beginning* to understand the height and the depth of God's love? I hope so, for I doubt that anything will stimulate one's growth in the Saviour more than a correct understanding and a true appreciation of this. Likewise, I doubt that anything will hinder it more than an incorrect understanding and a lack of appreciation of it. The central point that *must* be understood is this: our God *really, really* is a God of infinite love who seeks to pour out the blessings of omnipotence upon us. Furthermore, He is also a God of infinite wisdom who *always, always* knows what is best for us. All that is left for us to do is simply to admit our need of His mercy and grace and then to claim the fullness of His gift in Christ. I can assure you, reader, that these two simple acts—admitting our need and claiming Christ's fullness—will, by God's own providence, lead to a life of joyous upliftment and heartfelt obedience.

Remember, the key to growth is to bask in the light of God's love, and the key to being planted there is simply to be honest about one's own need and dependence, for this honesty, when coupled with the drawing power of God's lovingkindness, will eventually lead one to claim as one's own the fullness of His "unspeakable Gift."[9]

All the promises of God find their Yes in him.
That is why we utter the Amen through him,
to the glory of God.
(2 Corinthians 1:20 RSV)

· PRAISE THE LORD ·

---

1. Hannah Whitall Smith, *The Christian's Secret of a Happy Life* (Uhrichsville, Ohio:

Barbour, 1985), 179.

2. Ibid, 180.

3. Ibid., 178, 179.

4. Ibid., 181, 182.

5. Ibid., 158.

6. Ibid., 179, 180.

7. Ellen G. White, *Testimonies for the Church* (Boise, Idaho: Pacific Press Publishing Association, 1948), 5:740.

8. Ellen G. White, *The Desire of Ages* (Boise, Idaho: Pacific Press Publishing Association, 1940), 57.

9. Ibid., 26.

49

Sin is certainly not the most pleasant topic to discuss; nevertheless, we are all born into it, so we need to talk about it.

Most of us have too shallow an understanding of sin. If you, for example, were to ask any Adventist for a definition of sin, he or she would doubtless point you to 1 John 3:4 and say, "Sin is the transgression of the law." Now this is true, of course, but this definition does not begin to plumb the depths of sin's pollution in the human heart; it merely addresses its obvious, observable effects. As Adventists, we are all concerned with holding forth the perpetuity of God's law, and this definition of sin certainly lends itself to that end; nevertheless, we must come to a deeper understanding of sin if we are ever to be victors over that which desires us (Genesis 4:7).

First of all, I think we must all acknowledge that since we are, in fact, *born* into sin, our natural impulses toward God are those of rebellion and mistrust. For this reason, we are naturally incapable of receiving the blessings that our merciful and loving Father is always waiting to bestow upon us in Christ. We are always braced to *resist* the Almighty rather than to submit to Him. We are ever fearful of resigning ourselves completely to His providences, for we are inclined to think that such an act of total abandonment would surely expose us to embarrassment and humiliation. At the very least, we are inclined to think that we know better than anyone else what is best for us, so we would naturally rather remain in control of all the significant decisions in our lives instead of seeking another's guidance and direction (even if this Other happens to be God Himself).

But all of this must change, of course, if we are ever to know the Lord and subsequently to grow in our fellowship with Him. Each of us must confess, repent, and then take that decided and definite step of faith into the land of promise. In so doing, we will become planted in the blessed grace of God that alone can nurture and sustain our spiritual growth.

To return to a Scriptural definition of sin, the Bible provides, along with the definition found in 1 John 3:4, another in Romans 14:23. Here sin is characterized as "whatever does not proceed from faith." Thus, we see that sin comprises that entire realm of thought, feeling, and activity that is outside a faith relationship with the Almighty. This constitutes the fundamental essence of sin as it is experienced in the Christian life. We certainly see this in the opening chapters of the Genesis account where Adam and Eve endeavor to live a life of autonomy from their Creator (imagine!), and all of us see this in our own lives as well. We are ever prone toward restless wanderings from Him who would be our Father. We are ever prone to respond to His appeals with feelings of apprehension, suspicion, and doubt.

Have you not experienced this within yourself? Have you not experienced that pull that would inevitably lead you from your Saviour and your God?

Eventually, I think that each of us learns that the real issue in sin is an issue of trust and that its true essence in our lives can be revealed by questions such as, Why do I not depend fully upon the character and strength of the One who created and redeemed me? Why do I not rest my weight completely upon His promises and believe that He knows what is best for me?

Our tendency to *mis*trust God and to rebel against Him can never be fully explained, only confessed. This point is especially important nowadays, when every pathological tendency seems to be causally traced to some "dysfunction" in one's family. Now I do not deny the force of such influences, for they are certainly very real; I merely seek to point out that any explanation that is discovered along these lines is never a legitimate justification for sin. Furthermore, if you say, "Well, I'm this way because so and so member of my family was such and such a way," then, of course, this same explanation holds true for your family member as well (he or she simply points back to *his* or *her* family)—and on and on. This type of causal progression can end only with the ultimate first cause, which is, of course, God Himself—and we know that sin is not *His* fault.

But, you say, "No, it doesn't go back to God; it goes back only to Lucifer who rebelled in heaven."

Frankly, I believe that one way all of us have become especially adept at absolving ourselves from the full weight of condemnation that is due us is by our often rote explanations about the origin of sin. We talk mechanically about how Lucifer rebelled in heaven, about how Adam and Eve fell in the Garden of Eden. We point to Isaiah 14, to Ezekiel 28, to Genesis 3—we've got it all figured out. What we forget is that the Bible speaks of all manner of evil as proceeding from *my* heart (See Mark 7:21-23). Thus, for all practical purposes, sin originates in *me*, in the depths of *my* being, and, as such, it must simply be *confessed*. Had Lucifer not rebelled, had Adam and Eve not fallen, then I would *still* be the rebellious sinner at heart who mistrusts the Almighty and seeks to go it alone.

Do you believe this about yourself? Do you believe that—but for the grace of God in Christ—you are fully capable of doing all that Lucifer did, all that Adam and Eve did? Hear what the Word of the Lord says about each of us:

> *"There is none righteous, no, not one;*
> *There is none who understands;*
> *There is none who seeks after God.*
> *They have all gone out of the way;*
> *They have together become unprofitable;*

There is none who does good, no, not one."
"Their throat is an open tomb;
With their tongues they have practiced deceit";
"The poison of asps is under their lips";
"Whose mouth is full of cursing and bitterness."
"Their feet are swift to shed blood;
Destruction and misery are in their ways;
And the way of peace they have not known."
"There is no fear of God before their eyes."
(Romans 3:10-18, NKJV)

That passage is talking about you and me. *We* are the ones who don't understand. *We* are the ones who don't seek after God. (Do you believe that it is only by the Father's grace in Christ that you are even *drawn* to Him?) *We* are the ones whose throats are open tombs, whose tongues practice deceit, and whose feet are swift to shed blood. We—each one—stand condemned and deserving of death before the Almighty, for we have done over and over again what the Bible records Adam as having done only once in the Garden of Eden, and what it records our Saviour as having done not even once.

With regard to all of the causal reasoning that traces the roots of this sin to our ancestors, the Lord tells us in His Word what He thinks about this. The rebellious Israelites used to say, "The fathers have eaten sour grapes, and the children's teeth are set on edge." But through His prophet, the Lord responded, "You shall no longer use this proverb in Israel. But every one shall die for his own iniquity; every man who eats the sour grapes, his teeth shall be set on edge" (Jeremiah 31:29, 30; cf. Ezekiel 18, NKJV).

The Lord also informs us that our hearts are fully set to do evil—not because of any act on the part of our parents or our parents' parents—but rather "because sentence against an evil deed is not executed speedily" (Ecclesiastes 8:11, RSV). In other words, we continue to sin because, quite simply, we think we can get away with it. The mercy and forbearance of God—

which is intended, of course, to lead us to repentance—leads rather to a hardening of the heart in acts of wrongdoing and rebellion.

I do not mean to imply by this that our sinful nature is unrelated to our sinful ancestry. Lucifer did, in fact, rebel in heaven, and each of us is born with a fallen nature because he successfully enticed Adam and Eve to sin. My point is simply this: I do not believe that it is Lucifer's or anyone else's fault that you or I are susceptible to temptation. Furthermore, I believe that an inherent part of sin's pollution is the ongoing attempt to trace its blame to another. We see Adam and Eve doing this in the Garden of Eden, and each of us has a strong tendency to do likewise.

I do not deny the influence of one's parentage, for, as the Lord says, the effects of sin extend to the children and to the children's children "to the third and fourth generations" (Exodus 20:4, NKJV). My point is simply that our ancestry provides no justification for any conscious and willful departure from God's will, for as soon as one becomes aware of the sin in his or her life, just so soon may one lay hold of the Lord's all-sufficient grace in Christ by simply crying out to the Almighty for deliverance.

Sin originates in *me*, in *my* heart, and, as such, it cannot be justifiably traced to a source beyond myself. One might think of the matter in this way: the presence of sin in my life cannot be explained, for to explain it is to justify it. To explain it is to give a rational and coherent account for something that has no rational or coherent place in God's created order.[1] This point cannot be too strongly emphasized. We must not allow our Bible studies on the fall of Adam and Eve and the rebellion of Lucifer to deaden us to our own accountability with regard to sin. We should be appalled by its presence in our lives, for it is nothing less than a spurious intrusion that has *no* legitimate place in God's creation. Also, we must remember that when we talk about Adam and Eve or Lucifer, we are talking about *ourselves*. When we talk about what went on in *their* hearts, we are talking about what is presently going on in *our* hearts. Even if we do not take the final, irrevocable stand against the Almighty that Lucifer and his demons took, we still are guilty of the same proud, sinful thoughts of rebellion.

Another significant point about sin is this: the tendency in ourselves to try to explain the origin of our sinfulness cuts right to the very essence of justification by faith, for the very effort to explain our sin is really an effort to justify ourselves in our present state of rebellion. The truth of Scripture, however, is that we find our justification in Someone totally *extrinsic* to ourselves. Needless to say, this distinctively Christian truth is hard on proud, self-seeking flesh—we can hardly bear to hear it. It is far easier to concoct rationalization after rationalization than to just confess our sinfulness and admit that, in and of ourselves, we have no right standing before God.

To summarize, then: The only solution to the sin problem is God's act of grace in Christ, and the only way that we are able to lay hold of this is simply to *confess* our need. No "explanations" of any sort, no self-justifying rationalizations, just a humbling, soul-rending confession that acknowledges that the real problem is with *my* heart.

· PRAISE THE LORD ·

---

1. My thought on this topic was greatly clarified by G. E. Berkouer's chapter, "The Origin of Sin," in his work, *Sin*, trans. by Philip Holtrop (Grand Rapids: Eerdmans Pub. Co., 1971), pp. 11-26.

CHAPTER 8
SELF-DENIAL

Do you enjoy denying yourself? Do you believe that you are able to do this for the Lord?

The well-known text that exhorts us to exercise self-denial is the following:

> *If any man will come after me, let him deny himself,*
> *and take up his cross, and follow me.*
> *(Matthew 16:24)*

Now, what are we to make of this text? I have heard many interpret it something like this: *The Lord Jesus, as the incarnate Son of God, lived a life of consummate self-denial for me, so the least that I can do in return is to live a life of self-denial for Him.* The end result of this type of thinking is an individual who consciously denies himself (or herself) indulgences that he honestly and truly desires because he believes this is the way to "take up his cross" and be faithful to his Lord.

This approach has never worked for me. Never. Furthermore, I do not believe that this is what the Lord desires of us. Please allow me to explain.

First of all, imagine, if you will, a wife who says to her husband, "I have been faithful in all my vows to you, and I will continue to be faithful, but I wish for you to know that it is a very great cross for me, and I hardly know how to bear it." Or imagine a husband who says to his wife, "For your sake I deny myself of indulgences that I crave every day, and I promise you that I will gut it out and continue to

56

live this way for you as long as I live."[1]

Now I ask you, What person would accept such service from his or her spouse? Yet we expect the Lord to accept it from us. What we must understand is this: The Lord desires not merely a bride who is *faithful*, but also—and more importantly—a bride who is *in love*.[2] One who is in love will make any sacrifice for his or her beloved without considering it an act of self-denial. Thus must it be with us in all our relations with our Saviour and Lord, for if we are not fully enraptured with His glory and grace, then all of this "deny yourself" and "take up your cross" type of service is worthless. Furthermore, it is nothing less than a self-righteous affront to the Almighty.

I am not saying that acts of self-denial will not be performed; I am simply saying that they will not be perceived as such by the person performing them. Imagine, for example, a man who falls genuinely in love with a woman so that his experience is similar to that depicted in the Song of Solomon. This man is now transformed. A new power has taken hold that impels him to do things that formerly he would not do. From the world's perspective he is denying himself—but you could never convince *him* of this! From his own perspective he is simply basking in the light of romantic love, and he feels driven to do anything and everything for his beloved. In other words, from the standpoint of his own firsthand, conscious experience, he is dwelling in fullness, not lack. He does not feel as if he is being denied, but rather gratified. Do you see this?

The central point is this: On one level, one might legitimately say that a person in love is "denying herself" and "taking up her cross" for the sake of her beloved. But, of course, it is the power of love that is doing all the work, and as long as one simply *abides* in this power, then the work is essentially done *for* her, and she has absolutely no awareness of self-denial.

This is how our relationship with our Saviour and Lord should work, for He has done all the real work of self-denial, and if we simply abide in His fullness and His victory, then appropriate service will surely follow, and this service will comprise acts that we *really do* want to perform. In other words, we will not find ourselves in an unfulfilling grind where we are doing things that we know we *ought* to do, but do not *want* to do. Rather, we will find ourselves doing things that we *really want* to do! We will find ourselves springing up to meet the blessed will of God, for we will have found that it is only here that we find peace and security and rest. Our joy will be made full in service, and, like the man or the woman in love, we will find our greatest fulfillment in honoring Him who is the "chiefest among ten thousand" (Song of Solomon 5:10).

Of course, from the world's perspective, many of the acts we perform will appear self-denying in nature, and this will be so because the world embraces—not the new creation in Christ—but rather the carnal self that is enmity to the law of God. Thus, any act that flows from the fullness of one's relationship with the Almighty is an absolute mystery to the world, for it knows nothing of the power of the indwelling Christ. For this reason, we who are, in fact, empowered by Christ's fullness, appear to those of the world to be mysterious individuals who seem to live in basic denial of that most fundamental of human drives; namely, self-gratification. They are left in confusion and befuddlement by our behavior, since they know nothing save the insatiable clamorings of the carnal self.

I should point out that one could think about this whole matter of self-denial in the same way that I have suggested one think about *every* matter in the Christian walk; namely, one could think of it in terms of simply *claiming* perfect self-denial in Christ. Remember I suggested that you always ask the Lord to show you how anything that you seemingly have to *do* is accomplished *for you* in the life of your Saviour? Well, you can be certain this matter of self-denial is one such accomplishment; thus, it is yours for the asking. So, when you face this

exhortation to deny yourself, do not grit your teeth and resolve
to do it, for you will accomplish nothing but failure. Instead,
cry out to the Lord and confess that it simply is not in you to
deny your sinful, selfish, and greedy nature. Tell the Lord that
you are just too self-indulgent and uncaring to have regard for
anyone but yourself. Then hold up the mighty Lord Jesus and
tell the Almighty that *His* self-denial is your only hope. Then
claim it as your own, for it is surely the Lord's desire that you
do this (see 1 Corinthians 15:57). The Lord will surely bless
this act on your part. You will find yourself living out His fullness, and others will be saying, "How self-denying you are!"

One final point: The metaphor that our Lord Himself employs to represent self-denial is that of taking up a cross,
right? Now, do you happen to know how many biblical examples there are of someone doing this literally? There is
exactly one: that of Simon the Cyrenean. One cannot help
but thus ask, "What do we see in this case?" Well, first of
all, we see that the cross is given by the world, not the Lord.
When we look to the actual ordeal itself, we see Jesus, not
Simon, as the One who is taunted and mocked. We see Jesus,
not Simon, as the One who is beaten and scourged. And, of
course, we see Jesus, not Simon, as the One who is crucified. So I ask you, "How hard is it to carry a cross if the *other*
Person bears all the shame, the ridicule, and the pain?" Not
hard. So will it be for you—especially if you determine to
keep your eyes upon Christ (not yourself!) and realize that
just as soon as you confess to the Almighty that you are not
a "take up your cross" type of person, just so soon does He
lay all the associated pain and suffering of cross-bearing
upon His Son, the Lord Jesus.

Do you doubt this? If you do, then I would simply say, "Try
it and see."

The cross, the cross; lift it . . . and in the act of raising
it you will be astonished to find that it raises you, it sup-

ports you. In adversity, privation, and sorrow it will be a strength and a staff to you. You will find it all hung with mercy, compassion, sympathy, and inexpressible love.[3]

· **PRAISE THE LORD** ·

---

1. Hannah Smith expresses this thought in a similar way on page 168 of her work.
2. Francis Schaeffer expresses this thought in his book *The Church Before the Waiting World* (Downers Grove, Ill.: InterVarsity Press, 1971), 60.
3. Ellen G. White, *Testimonies for the Church* (Boise, Idaho: Pacific Press Publishing Assn., 1948) 2:47.

CHAPTER 9

THE·JOY·OF·OBEDIENCE

The topic of obedience is very similar to the topic of self-denial. However, the topic of joyful obedience is so important that I wish to devote an entire chapter to it.

I will begin this chapter with a very significant quote from the Spirit of Prophecy:

> "The man who attempts to keep the commandments of God from a sense of obligation merely—because he is required to do so—will never enter into the joy of obedience. He does not obey. When the requirements of God are accounted a burden because they cut across human inclination, we may know that the life is not a Christian life. True obedience is the outworking of a principle within. "[1]

If Seventh-day Adventist Christians truly believed this, then most misunderstanding with regard to the life of faith would be corrected. The significant point is this: true Christians endeavor to do the will of the Lord because they *truly desire* to do this; they *truly desire* to please Him—just like a bride who is in love with her bridegroom. This is what it means to be born again. This is what it means to be converted. This is what it means to have Jesus in your heart.

Now the obvious questions that arise are these: What if I do *not* desire to do the will of the Lord? What if I do *not* desire to please Him? What if His requirements *are* accounted a burden because they cut across my inclination? What then?

Well, one thing is certain: If you are one who is compelled to ask the foregoing questions, then you have not yet entered into the joy of obedience, and your life is thus not a *Christian* life. Please understand that this is what the prophet of the Lord says: your life is not a *Christian* life.

Of course, it makes *sense* that your life is not a Christian life, for a Christian life is simply a life in which Christ *lives*, and if your inclination is not to do the will of the Lord, then Christ obviously does not live within you. Do you see this?

So, what should you do? Well, I hope it is clear that the one thing you should *not* do is to try to be more externally obedient, for it is not external obedience that you need, but rather the *joy* of obedience.

And how do you get this? Like anything else in the life of faith, you claim it in Christ.

Now, what you will find when you claim this joy in Christ is that the Lord will *lift* you into it. He will not beat you down, for Christ has already borne all of that chastisement for you. To repeat: The Lord will *lift* you. He will *lift* you into His joy.

Now, *how* will the Lord lift you into His joy? Well, one thing is virtually certain: The means that He will employ will be *within* the fellowship of believers, *within* the body of Christ. In other words, the Lord will open a door (or doors) for you to become involved in a prayer group or a Bible study or a local ministry—*something* within the body of Christ. You will then reap the joy from this involvement—pure and holy joy. And this joy will become, as the Bible says, your strength (see Nehemiah 8:10). You will no longer find that you must force yourself to do the will of the Lord; on the contrary, doing His bidding will become your very food and drink. It will become that which nourishes and sustains you, and you would think as much of not indulging in the Lord's blessed will as you would think of not eating or drinking. Also, you will find rest in the will of the Lord, and this rest will be the sweetest that you have ever known—rest that continually refreshes and re-news.

Now the one obstacle that will prevent all of this from tak-ing place is your natural shame of fellowship in the Lord Jesus. This topic of shame is certainly a delicate one, but there is no doubt in my mind that all of us must acknowledge its pres-ence within us with openness and honesty. That is, we must all come to the point where we are able to openly and hon-estly confess the shame of the Lord Jesus that is quite natu-rally in our sinful hearts, for if we refuse to do this, then, like the spiritually unconverted Peter, we will surely deny our Lord when the scorn and reproach of the world falls upon us, and in so doing, we will miss the blessings and the joy that come only from fellowship in His body. (I will explain this concept of shame further in the next chapter.)

The one who faithfully obeys is ever feasting upon the blessed will of God. He (or she) may indeed do things the world would consider hard or strenuous, but he is *impelled* to do them. He is driven by the very power of omnipotence, and he would no more think of not doing the will of the Lord than he would think of not saving his beloved spouse from an onrush-ing train.

Please think for a moment about a man who is in the pre-dicament of having to save his beloved spouse (or child) from an onrushing train. Such an individual might indeed have to exert. He might have to stretch and strain. He might even have to risk his own life. Nevertheless, when the moment of such an occurrence arrives, he does not stop to weigh the cost; on the contrary, he merely *responds* to the predicament at hand with determination and power. When the living Christ lives in you by faith, you will respond to divine promptings in just this way.

Now I could write much more about this topic of joyful obedience, but I would rather defer to the prophet of the Lord in this area. I hope the following selection of inspired statements will convince you that anything less than joyful and heartfelt obedience is one of the clearest signs that something is very wrong with your profession of faith.

We must not trust at all to ourselves nor to our good works; but when as erring, sinful beings we come to Christ, we may find rest in His love. God will accept every one that comes to Him trusting wholly in the merits of a crucified Saviour. *Love springs up in the heart*. There may be no ecstasy of feeling, but there is an abiding, peaceful trust. *Every burden is light*, for the yoke which Christ imposes is easy. *Duty becomes a delight*, and *sacrifice a pleasure*. The path that before seemed shrouded in darkness becomes *bright* with beams from the Sun of Righteousness. *This* is walking in the light as Christ is in the light. [2]

Looking unto Jesus we obtain brighter and more distinct views of God, and by beholding we become changed. Goodness, love for our fellow men, becomes our *natural instinct*. [3]

All true obedience comes from the *heart*. It was heart work with Christ. And if we consent, He will so identify Himself with our thoughts and aims, so blend our hearts and minds into conformity to His will, that when obeying Him we shall be but carrying out *our own impulses*. The will, refined and sanctified, will find its *highest delight* in doing *His* service. [4]

Now, what does the Word of God have to say about joyful obedience?

Well, first of all, consider the apostle Paul. In the sixth chapter of his second letter to the Corinthians, he chronicles some of the many types of suffering that he had endured for the sake of the gospel. He speaks of himself as being "in tribulations, in needs, in distresses, in stripes, in imprisonments, in tumults, in labors, in sleeplessness, in fastings"(2 Corinthians 6:4, 5, NKJV). Did all of this make Paul sorrowful? Well, yes—sometimes. But hear what he says: "Sorrowful, yet *always rejoicing*" (2 Corinthians 6:10, NKJV). Yes—rejoicing. This is what the Word of the Lord says about the experience of Paul. Truly, anyone who believes that this exemplary apostle was one who joylessly endured all of his hardships for the sake of Christ knows nothing of the substance and the reality of the Christian life. Indeed, Paul himself, after listing the central quality of love as the first fruit of the Spirit, immediately lists *joy* as the second (see Galatians 5:22).

Also, the psalmist says,

> **I delight to do thy will, O my God: yea,**
> **thy law is within my heart.**
> **(Psalm 40:8)**

Now one might contend that this scripture is describing the Lord Jesus, and, of course, it is. But one must always remember that the mighty Lord Jesus is fully *ours* by faith. Thus, when He lives in us by His Spirit, *we, too*, will delight to do the Lord's will, because His law will be written in *our* hearts (see Hebrews 8:10).

I hope you will not settle for anything less than a life of joyful obedience, for if you do, then you will be settling for something less than being a Christian. If you are not presently experiencing the Lord's joy, then ask the Holy Spirit to reveal the reason to you. He will. And when He does, be willing to accept responsibility for whatever He brings to your remembrance. Also, be willing to humbly confess any sinful tendencies that surface. If you feel *un*willing to accept any responsibility or to confess any sin, then confess *that*. Confess your unwillingness. The key to victory in this area (as in any other) is simply to acknowledge the truth and then to cry out to the

Lord for deliverance. He will meet you right where you are. And He will not cease to work until He has lifted you into the fullness of His abundant life.

The only thing that will hinder this process is your sinful flesh, and, of course, this sinful flesh "clings so closely"(Hebrews 12:1, RSV). Now if you fear that you are just too wayward and perverse to be lifted into the Lord's joy because your sinful flesh will surely hinder this blessed work, then confess *that*. In other words, confess to the Lord that you would like for Him to lift you into His joy, but you know yourself all too well, and you thus realize that you will doubtless resist Him at every step and thus thwart His beautiful and blessed plan for your life. Just confess that. Then cry out for deliverance. You will soon discover that the Lord is able to lift you beyond even the seemingly uncontrollable clamorings of your sinful flesh.

Do you doubt that the Lord can do all this for you? If you do, then confess *that*. Again, the Lord will meet you right where you are. Satan wants nothing more than to convince you that you cannot receive the Lord's joy. He would have you believe that obedience to the Lord will forever be a monotonous grind for a sinner like you. Nothing could be farther from the truth. The Lord will reach you right where you are, and, with His help, you will surely experience the blessedness of a life of obedience. You will discover *firsthand* that such a life is one of buoyancy and ease, one of joy and peace.

I could write much more about joyful obedience. Surely you cannot continue to doubt that this is God's will for you, can you? If you do, then you will go on living a life of joyless servitude, and, like the elder brother in the parable of the prodigal son, you will become angry and resentful whenever you see the Father give His joyful fullness to a redeemed sinner (see Luke 15:28). You, like the elder brother in this parable, must realize that *all* that the Father has is yours (see verse 31), and that you are able—*right now*—to claim the fullness of His joy in your service. Truly, the Father is not pleased until you, like David, have drunk deeply at the fount of His blessing and can thus truthfully exclaim, "My cup runneth over"(Psalm 23:5).

Trust the Almighty to lift you into His joy. (And if you feel that you *cannot* trust Him, then confess *that!*)

> ***Thanks be to God,***
> ***that you who were once slaves of sin***
> ***have become obedient from the heart***
> ***To the standard of teaching to which you were***
> ***committed.***
> ***(Romans 6:17, RSV)***

·　　P R A I S E　　T H E　　L O R D　　·

---

1. Ellen White, *Christ's Object Lessons*. (Boise, Idaho: Pacific Press Publishing Assn., 1941), 91.

2. ____. *Selected Messages*. (Hagerstown. Md., Review and Herald Publishing Assn., 1958) 1:354, emphasis supplied.

3. ____. *Christ's Object Lessons*, 355, emphasis supplied.

4. ____. *The Desire of Ages*. (Boise, Idaho: Pacific Press, 1940), 688, emphasis supplied.

CHAPTER 10

THE · LAW · AND · THE · GOSPEL

I mentioned in the previous chapter that the only obstacle that would prevent one from being lifted into the joy of the Lord Jesus is the natural shame of Him that exists in our sinful hearts. I would now like to elaborate upon this topic more fully since I believe it is such a critically important area of the Christian walk.

First of all, in order to give this discussion a scriptural basis, please look to the second chapter of the book of Galatians. Here we find Peter and Barnabas condemned with regard to the gospel. Now, I believe that all of us understand what it means to be condemned with regard to the law: This amounts to the breaking of one of the Ten Commandments. We usually think of condemnation with regard to the gospel in the same way, but Peter and Barnabas are here condemned—not for breaking a specific commandment (although, as always, one could surely find one that applies)—but rather for denying their fellowship with the Gentile believers in Antioch. The apostle Paul writes under inspiration that such an act on their part meant that "they were not straightforward about the truth of the gospel" and thus "stood condemned" (Galatians 2:14, 11, RSV).

Here we find one of the most difficult tests for the Christian: Will you allow yourself to be identified with the Lord Jesus and His body? The victory that the Almighty freely gives to us is here and nowhere else. Thus, if you and I seek to come into *possession* of this victory, then we must allow ourselves to be identified with the Lord's body, and we must allow this identification to take place in a world that hates the Lord and all that He represents.

If you examine the account that is written in the second chapter of Galatians, you will see that the individuals whom Peter feared were those of the "circumcision party" (Galatians 2:12). In other words, Peter withdrew from fellowshiping with the uncircumcised Gentile believers because he was afraid of those Jews who believed that all must be circumcised. Circumcision was the outward sign of one's consecration to the Lord in a covenant commitment, and the Jews had come to regard their participation in this ritual as a virtual guarantee of their right standing with God and thus as an assurance of His favor. The real necessity in this covenant relationship, however (as the apostle Paul points out), was inward, not outward. That is, the real necessity was spiritual conversion, the reception of the regenerating power of the Holy Spirit. In short, the real necessity was "circumcision of the heart" (Deuteronomy 30:6).

He is not a real Jew who is one outwardly,
nor is true circumcision something
external and physical.
He is a Jew who is one inwardly,
and real circumcision is a matter of the heart,
spiritual and not literal.
(Romans 2:28, 29, RSV)

69

Just as the Jews of our Lord's day focused on outward forms rather than the inward condition of their hearts, so do we. It is really quite easy to slip into a Christian lifestyle where one is outwardly quite upstanding but is inwardly as resistant to the Lord and His Spirit as the most vile of sinners. Of course, this type of "Christian" experience merely feeds one's sinful pride and effectively prevents one from acknowledging his or her deep need of the Lord's healing grace. It also allows us to cling to our shame of the Lord Jesus Christ since our preoccupation with the outward forms of religion usually results in a life of religious "busyness" that effectively insulates us from having to come face to face with this. Unfortunately, however, we usually are unable to detect when we are in this legalistic state, for our hearts truly are "deceitful above all things, and desperately wicked" (Jeremiah 17:9). The important point for our present purposes is this: The Bible shows quite clearly that individuals who cling to the outward forms of religion and do not openly and honestly confess their need of Christ stand condemned with regard to the gospel of grace.

Now, I could certainly write much about my own entanglement in this legalistic and self-righteous condition, but I will, instead, proceed with this discussion of the law and the gospel.

As I have stated, the test for you or for me will not amount to having to keep God's law, for our Lord Jesus has already passed that test, and the Bible is quite clear that His life of perfect obedience and submission is given to us freely as a gift. For this reason, the law, as such, drops out of the salvation equation. Now, I do not mean to imply by this that believers in the Lord should not be commandment keepers, for we should be commandment keepers (see 1 John 2:4; 5:3). I seek merely to point out that this keeping of the commandments is merely the fruit and not the root of our salvation. In other words, the basis of our right standing with God, as well as our salvation experience, is not the law or our keeping of the law, but rather the finished work of our Lord Jesus Christ. This is such a simple truth, yet it is such an important and powerful one. It is also one that is very easily overlooked in our everyday life. Frankly, I have no doubt that we often look beyond this powerful truth, and, in so doing, we lose sight of the completeness of Christ's victory in our behalf; thus, we get an entirely wrong idea of the mechanics of salvation. In short, we begin to focus on the law and our keeping of the law instead of focusing on the Lord, and we forget that the words of Paul that were addressed to the self-righteous Jews of his day apply with equal force to ourselves: "You who boast in the law, do you dishonor God by breaking the law?" (Romans 2:23, RSV).

Please understand that since Christ is given to us freely as a gift, there is no need for us to focus on the law apart from Him. That is, there is no need for us to focus on the law in the impersonal or the abstract, for if one has become convicted of sin and subsequently drawn to Christ as the only hope of salvation, then the primary *function* of the law has been fulfilled (see Romans 3:20 and Galatians 3:24). It continues to be important in the Christian walk, of course, but only as a "custodian" that continues to lead us to Christ so that we may be justified by faith (Galatians 3:24, RSV). The bottom line, I believe, is this: We must all come to the realization that the law was given for the restraint and conviction of the old man of sin, not the growth and nurturance of the new creation in Christ.

I believe this point can be taken one step farther. That is, I believe that anyone who focuses on the law and the keeping of the law apart from its fulfillment in Christ is one who, like the Jews of the circumcision party, has not fully embraced the truth of the gospel. In short, I believe that he is one who has no living experience with Christ as His Saviour from sin, for if he did, then he would be focusing upon Him, and he would be trying to share with others the peace and the love that our Lord has given to him. Needless to say, it is the blot of arrogance and pride in our sinful hearts that keeps us from experiencing the joy of salvation. Such pride desires to be independent of any higher authority—even if that authority happens to be the Creator and Redeemer Himself. If we surrender to the dominion of this sinful pride, then we naturally take offense at One Who could live a life of perfect moral dependence and submission, and we thus miss the blessing of those who would take no offense at Him (Matthew 11:6).

I hope you realize that the principal source of pain and frustration for the born-again believer is not that individuals resist the demands of the law; rather, the principal source of pain and frustration for the born-again believer is that individuals resist the gospel of Christ. In other words, those who have been born into the vitalizing power and saving grace of the gospel are hurt and saddened most of all by seeing those whom the Lord loves resist the mercy and grace that is fully able to restore and renew them in His image.

Do you not experience this frustration? Do you not experience the sadness and the exasperation of telling those who have been made wretched and miserable by sin about the Saviour and then have them say, "No thanks; I'll go it alone"?

The real issue in this matter of the law, the gospel, and the shame of Jesus that exists in our sinful hearts can be seen very plainly by observing the Jews' response to the suffering of our Saviour on Calvary. Here we see the self-righteous Jews (those who clung to the outward forms of religion with rigid detail) looking upon a crucified Saviour (He who had no regard for such hypocrisy and who mingled with the common folk with perfect liberty and ease). Said the Jews: "If he be the King of Israel, let him now come down from the cross, and we will believe him" (Matthew 27:42). This is the world's attitude toward our Lord. If He will come down from the cross and be the kind of king of which the world feels it is worthy (one who possesses a dignified outward form and a self-important manner), then it will believe. But to see a Man who claims to be God hanging on a cross is to be convicted of sin, and conviction of sin is the one thing that this "I'm OK, you're OK" world wants nothing of. Far easier is it to project one's shame of oneself onto the perfect Lamb of God than to face it like a man and to bow down at the foot of the cross in confession and repentance.

I have no doubt that the test for you and for me will be one of allowing ourselves to be identified with that body of believers who proclaim the authority of a crucified and risen Lord in a world that treats Him as the perfect scapegoat for its sin.

Now, along these lines of proclaiming the authority of a crucified and risen Lord in this world, I think it is fair to say that most of us think of this proclamation as it applies to ourselves as our "testimony." In other words, when I *do* proclaim the authority of a crucified and risen Lord, when I *do* tell of what He has done for me in my life, then I am, in short, giving my testimony. This seems true, right?

Well, the Bible speaks of those who overcame the devil, and inspiration reveals that they have done this by "the blood of the Lamb and by the word of their testimony" (Revelation 12:11).

Now the "blood of the Lamb" part of this victory was obviously accomplished by Christ, and it is this, of course, that opens the door for us to enter into a joyous fellowship with the Father and the Son through a simple confession of our need. The only part that is left for us is "the word of their testimony." The significant point, I believe, is this: If we will simply consent to take our focus off our own experience with all of its perceived struggles and trials and consent to bear witness to the experience of the Lord Jesus Christ (to proclaim His authority in this world of sin and death), then we will find ourselves lifted above all the perplexity and bondage of our own lives into the glorious victory that should be His alone. He has already won the victory over all sin and temptation, and when we simply take Him at His word in this area and then act on this truth by proclaiming His victory in our behalf to a sin-bound world (regardless of the present testimony of our own experience), then we will invariably find that His victory is ours.

I could write so much about how important this area of witnessing has been in my own experience, and I cannot begin to tell you how very, very thankful I am for the bold testimony I believe the Lord has given me for His Son. Truly, I have no doubt that it is this testimony—probably more than anything else—that has brought me my present measure of victory over sin and the devil.

Now I hope you understand that if you are presently struggling with some long-cherished sin in your life, then the real issue might have nothing at all to do with gaining greater insight about the sin itself (this might simply be where the evil one is keeping your attention focused so that you will not secure the reality of Christ's victory). On the contrary, the real issue might be one of gaining greater insight about why you are ashamed of the Lord Jesus Christ and thus will not witness to His glory. (I write this as one who has had to plumb the depths in this area of his own sinful heart, and who continues to have to do this on occasion.) If you doubt that what I am writing is true, then do the following: Refuse to wage a sterner battle against the sin in your life, and, instead, simply confess to the Lord that you are ashamed of His Son and ask Him to reveal the reasons for this and to give you a bold testimony for Christ. See if matters do not begin to change in your life. I can assure you that the mighty Lord Jesus has no desire that you be bound by sin and the devil, and if you will but trust the Father to give you a bold testimony for His Son, then His very own Word guarantees that you will find deliverance.

It guarantees it.

> *They overcame him by the blood of the Lamb,*
> *and by the word of their testimony.*
> *(Revelation 12:11)*

So the real issue in your or my salvation is not one of battling with this or that temptation or inner struggle, for battles on this level are reflective of a self-absorbed individual who refuses to look to the Lord to be saved. Rather, the real issue is simply this: Will you witness for the Lord Jesus Christ?

Will you?

I can assure you that if you will do just that, then you will immediately begin to secure the reality of His victorious life in your own Christian walk.

> *Whosoever . . . shall confess me before men,*
> *him will I confess also before my Father*
> *which is in heaven.*
> *But whosoever shall deny me before men,*
> *him will I also deny before my Father*
> *which is in heaven.*
> *(Matthew 10:32, 33)*

> *Whosoever therefore shall be ashamed*
> *of me and of my words*
> *in this adulterous and sinful generatio;,*
> *of him also shall the Son of man be ashamed,*
> *when he cometh in the glory of his Father*
> *with the holy angels.*
> *(Mark 8:38)*

Trust the Lord to give you a bold testimony in this most important of areas. And remember: If your sinful heart condemns you as you begin to bear witness to our Saviour before this sin-loving world (as mine surely did when I began to do this), then understand that the Lord still accepts your testimony before men and is honored by it, for His Word says,

> *If our heart condemn us,*
> *God is greater than our heart,*
> *and knoweth all things.*
> *(1 John 3:20)*

In other words, if you are bearing witness to the Lord Jesus Christ in a conscious and deliberate attempt to mock the Father and the Son, then the Lord is able to read this intent of your heart, and He will, of course, turn away from such a lying testimony. But if you recognize that the mighty Lord Jesus truly is your only hope of salvation, and if you sincerely desire to honor Him even though your heart is filled to the brim with pollution, hypocrisy, and unbelief, then you can act on this righteous impulse from the Lord and know that He accepts it even though the evil one is condemning you through it all and calling you a lying hypocrite.

As a final point, I would remind you of this: The Lord Jesus was One who, for the sake of the joy that was set before Him, endured the cross, despising the shame (see Hebrews 12:2). We must do likewise. That is, we must despise the shame of the cross of Christ that exists quite naturally in our hearts. And if you will but confess this shame openly and honestly to the Lord, then He will give you a hatred of it (I believe this is implied in the promise of Genesis 3:15). He will also give you a bold testimony for His Son. You will thus find yourself proclaiming the name of the Lord Jesus Christ, and you will likewise find yourself abiding in His victory and His joy.

· PRAISE THE LORD ·

CHAPTER 11 CONFESSION AND·THE·WILL

If we cannot do anything that will assist in our salvation, then what, pray tell, does the Lord require of us in order that we may be saved?

I would say only this:

Admit to our helplessness.

Admit to our need.

Or to put matters into biblical terms: confess.

If one were to endeavor to capture the essence of our role in salvation in but one word, then the word honesty would be my choice, for if one is merely honest, then he (or she) will be driven to do the one thing that is required for salvation: confess his helplessness and need.

"But what does all of this have to do with 'Confession and the Will'?" you may ask. Well, plenty, because there is a very important connection between a Christian act of confession and a Christian act of will. This connection is one that must be understood if one is to be successful in the life of faith.

Imagine that you have recently become very serious about overcoming a certain sin in your life. Now, if this were true, then what would you think of doing? If you are like the vast majority of Christians with whom I have spoken, you would doubtless think of exercising a greater resolve to do the Lord's will. In other words, you would think about choosing (with more tenacity than previously, of course) to put away the sin in your life and to serve the Lord more fully and completely. Now, whenever you do something like this, I believe you are doomed to failure, for I believe you will always find that all such resolutions and promises—though made with the utmost sincerity—are impossible to keep.

The sanctuary services of the ancient Israelites illustrate why the way of resolve is not the way of victory. These services were a symbolic demonstration of the plan of redemption; thus, by looking to them, we can learn much about the role of Christ as our sacrifice and High Priest, and we can also learn much about our own role in salvation.

So, what do we see when we look to the sanctuary services? Well, first of all, we see that there were sin and guilt offerings. These were sacrifices that were offered when one had sinned before the Lord and had thus broken one's covenant with Him. These offerings required that the sinner bring an animal without blemish to the altar of burnt offering. The sinner was then required to place his hands on the head of the animal, confess his sin, and kill the animal (see Leviticus 4:1–6:7).

The innocent animal without blemish represented Christ, of course, and this whole service pointed forward to (among other things) His sacrificial death on Calvary. By confessing one's sin over the animal and then slaying it, the guilt of the sin was symbolically transferred to the innocent offering, and then, via the blood and the priest's ministration, to the sanctuary.

When individuals had sinned, they were required to confess their need before any sort of forgiveness and atonement could be effected. Thus, the order of events was something like this: (1) honesty before the Lord, (2) confession of sin and need, and (3) forgiveness and atonement.

Now all of that seems very sensible and straightforward, does it not? But now imagine this: You have sinned before the Lord. You bring your sin offering, make your confession, slay the animal, and then the priest performs the appropriate ministry. You are thus forgiven your sin (which is to say that the guilt of it is symbolically transferred to the sanctuary). You now go back to your tent and resolve never to do that sinful act again. Seems reasonable enough, right? Well, according to the terms of the covenant, this was not allowed. In other words, if you had reached the point of resolving never to do such and such a sinful act again, then you were required to bring yet another animal to the altar of burnt offering, lay your hands upon this innocent offering, and then slay it before the Lord. The point, I believe, is this: Voluntary acts of worship and consecration—like mandatory acts of acknowledgment of sin—required a blood sacrifice and a confession of need (see Leviticus 1; 6:8-13).

Now the implication of this seems quite clear; namely, one cannot resolve—by any personal act of will—to commit oneself to the Lord. Rather, any commitment to the Lord must be preceded by an act of confession, an act where one acknowledges one's need of something that he or she cannot supply.

"But," you say, "one cannot successfully choose to put away the sin in his (or her) life before he comes to the Lord, but after he comes, then he can."

Well, if you believe this, then please notice that the Israelites who were required to make these sacrifices of commitment and consecration ("burnt offerings," as they were called) were those who already stood in a covenant relation with God. In other words, they were not heathen unbelievers who knew not the power of the Almighty. On the contrary, they had witnessed His power in the Exodus from Egypt (symbolizing, of course, one's deliverance from the bondage of sin). And yet, despite their deliverance from Egyptian darkness, despite their justified standing before the Holy Shekinah in their midst (which, of course, represented the very presence of God), they were still required to offer a blood sacrifice and to confess their state of need before any voluntary act of devotion or surrender would be acceptable to the Lord.

So, to summarize: In the sacrifice for forgiveness of sin, the Israelites would come to the altar realizing that a perfect life was something they could not supply; thus, they would offer the lamb without blemish as a substitute perfect life that they could claim by faith and that would, of course, point forward to the Lamb of God who takes away the sin of the world. The important point for our present purposes is this: In the presentation of this offering, all that the Israelites would supply was a confession of need.

Now, in the sacrifice for consecration or commitment, we see a striking parallel. That is, the Israelites would come to the altar in this instance realizing that there was something they could not supply. They would offer a lamb or other animal without blemish as a substitute that they could claim by faith and that pointed forward to the Lamb of God. The only difference, I believe, is that whereas in the sin offering the focus of the sacrifice is the representation of a perfectly righteous life as a basis for forgiveness, in the burnt offering the focus of the sacrifice is the representation of a perfectly surrendered life that provided a basis for consecration.

It is significant to note along these lines that the procedure outlined for the burnt offering (that literally means "ascent") dictated that all of the offering except the blood be burned and ascend in smoke. It is also significant, I believe, to note that the Lord stated that this "ascent" produced a "sweet aroma" (Leviticus 1:13, 17, NKJV). This description of a "sweet aroma" seems to be a very appropriate characterization of a symbol representing a perfectly devoted and surrendered life. I must also say that I honestly wonder if anything other than a perfectly devoted and surrendered life could be justifiably characterized as producing a "sweet aroma" to a pure and holy God. For these reasons, I believe this "ascent" (the burnt offering) represents none other than the total and complete devotion of Christ's life, a life which was perfectly surrendered to His Father's will.

The important point from all of this is that in the presentation of the burnt offering, all that the Israelites could supply was a confession of need. In other words, just as confession was, in the sin offering, the only condition required to bring forgiveness, so was it also, in the burnt offering, the only condition required to bring a willingness to serve the Almighty.

In the New Testament, the portion of Scripture that is most significant in relation to the role of confession and the will is Romans, chapters six through eight. Here Paul gives a beautiful and intensely personal account of the life of righteousness by faith in Christ. One could easily write an entire book about these three chapters; thus, I certainly make no claim to give any sort of final analysis here. Nevertheless, I believe it is clear here that the way of the will (Paul's struggles in chapter seven) is not the way of victory in the Christian walk. I believe it is equally clear that Paul is speaking in this chapter as a converted man. That is, he is speaking as one who is under conviction by the Holy Spirit and as one who is seeking to follow this conviction by living a holy life that is pleasing to God. (Unconverted persons definitely do not seek to live lives that are pleasing to God; indeed, many would not even consent that His commandments are "good"–Romans 7:12.)

Now the obvious question is this: How is Paul delivered from this struggle and defeat that result in his exclaiming, "O wretched man that I am"? (Romans 7:24). Paul answers this in the very next chapter, and here we see him writing–not about willing–but rather about walking. He writes that the righteous requirement of the law is fulfilled in those who walk according to the Spirit of life in Christ Jesus (Romans 8:1-4).

One might justifiably inquire, "But what does it mean to walk according to the Spirit of life in Christ Jesus?" Well, Paul writes to the Colossians that it amounts to nothing more than what it took to receive the Spirit of life in Christ Jesus, for his words to those at Colossae are, "As ye have therefore received Christ Jesus the Lord, so walk ye in him" (Colossians 2:6).

How did you initially receive Christ Jesus as Saviour and Lord? By resolving to do so? Or by confessing that you could not do so? Did you not receive Christ after you had finally reached the breaking point in your own experience and thus realized–possibly for the first time–that all your promises and resolutions were like ropes of sand? In short, did you not receive Him through a confession of need? The Scriptures say, "So walk ye in Him."

I will now ask you to imagine once again that you have become very serious about overcoming the sin in your life. I would then suggest (on the basis of the Scripture that we have just studied) the following course of action: Instead of trying to choose to serve God or to exercise your will in the right direction, confess instead. That is, rather than setting your mind and your will to do that which you believe the Lord is leading you to do, confess instead that you cannot do it. I believe that this one simple act of honest confession will result in a dramatic change for the better in your Christian experience.

Now you might say, "Wait a minute. The Lord does require that we do certain things in our lives. We can't just go around confessing our inability all the time like a bunch of cowards or weaklings. Besides, the Spirit of Prophecy says that 'Everything depends upon the right action of the will' (*Steps to Christ*, 47)."

I believe that everything I have written in this chapter is fully consistent with this well-known statement from the Spirit of Prophecy. I believe that the obvious intent of the statement is that one must surrender the will to God, and this is the precise point I am trying to make. What I am arguing against is not the Spirit of Prophecy statement itself, but rather the misinterpretation and misapplication of it by some in our church. For by misinterpreting and misapplying this statement, I believe many have been left with the mistaken impression that the condition of salvation is a personal act of will rather than an honest confession of need.

I wonder whether anything can lead a person to hopelessness and discouragement more quickly than the mistaken belief that the assurance of his or her salvation depends upon the power of his or her will. If salvation is truly a gift, then it must simply be received. And the only condition to receiving something is confessing one's need of it. (See Appendix B for an in-depth analysis of this Spirit of Prophecy statement in its context.)

Now, to return to the issue of whether or not we can go around confessing our inability all the time like a bunch of cowards or weaklings, I would say that I believe we can. Furthermore, I believe this is the only way that the "doing gets done," so to speak, in the Christian walk.

Now those who believe they are not cowards or weaklings would probably contend that confessing their inability all the time will not get the doing done. They might argue that simply setting one's mind to do the right thing and then trusting in God to supply the needed grace will lead to right action.

I certainly would not want anyone to think that I am arguing that it is wrong to set one's mind to do what is right. My point is simply this: The whole process of setting out to do what is right is merely an exercise in self-righteousness and self-deception unless one has first received the mind of Christ, for only our Saviour has the moral integrity and the spiritual fortitude to commit to an upright path and then to follow through, come what may. Also, when one receives the mind of Christ, one receives the mind of Him who loved righteousness and hated iniquity (see Hebrews 1:9), and who delighted to do His Father's will because His law was within His heart (see Psalm 40:8). In short, when one receives the mind of Christ, one receives the desire to serve the Lord.

For this reason, any commitment to do what is right that is brought forth by an honest confession of need will always result in an individual's receiving Christ's willingness to serve His Father. It will never result in an individual's being left in the position of having to "will" to serve our Father in Heaven while his or her heart is far from Him. (As I pointed out in the chapter on self-denial, such "service" is nothing less than a self-righteous affront to the Almighty.)

If an individual decides to "gut it out," so to speak, and resolves to "will" to serve the Father while his or her heart is yet far from Him, then such an act of gritty resolve will serve only to harden that individual's heart against the truth of the gospel.

I will tell you how this whole process takes place for me. Whenever I become convicted by the Lord that I must overcome a certain sin in my life or do a certain work, then the knowledge of my own weakness and insufficiency looms up before me, and I feel driven to honestly confess before the Almighty that I am an inadequate instrument. I thus cry out for deliverance in Christ, and I invariably find that His blessed peace then floods my soul, and I suddenly feel empowered by the living water that proceeds from the throne of God. The important point, I believe, is this: The whole process begins with a confession of need, not a personal act of will. Both the power to choose to do right and the power to follow through with this choice come only after one has confessed his (or her) need and thus opened the door to receive Christ. This is the key—receiving Christ. For when one receives Him, then one receives the omnipotent power of *His* will.

One could think of the entire matter in this way: Salvation is a process that is effected by faith, not by resolve. In other words, everything in the salvation process hinges on your simply taking the Lord at His Word; it does not hinge on any personal act of will. It never hinges upon any personal act of will. It is always by faith—always. And faith is simply a gift that one receives when one confesses his need to the Lord.

Another way that one could think about the matter is this: It was the will that became fallen in the Garden of Eden, for Adam and Eve did nothing less than to choose to disobey God. Now until this corruptible puts on incorruption, our only connection with an unfallen will is by faith in Christ. In other words, we never reach a point of "holy flesh" where we can rely on our own wills for anything in the salvation process. Our reliance must always be upon Christ (for everything!), and the only part that we contribute to the salvation process is a simple acknowledgment of our great need.

With regard to this matter of personal acts of will, please allow me to ask you something: Do you really think that you have even once chosen to serve the Almighty and then followed through with your decision to the extent that your resolution and His holiness required? I haven't. Not even once. And, furthermore, I regard all those "choices" on my part to be simply a part of the learning process the Lord has taken me through in order to teach me that I cannot rely on the "power" of my will. I believe the Lord has shown me that the only true foundation on which I can safely rest is His merciful act of grace in Christ, and the way that I lay hold of this is by a simple and honest confession of need.

I should mention that if I had thought (when I really hit bottom) that everything in my salvation depended on the right action of my will, then I would surely have packed it in. Why? Well, because the very problem was with my will. It was, quite simply, in bondage to Satan. How could I use it to choose to serve God?

I should mention also that nothing has changed in my personal assessment of this matter now that I have grown in God's grace. That is, the problem is still with my will, and if I were to think that everything (or even anything) in my salvation depended upon its right action, then I would still pack it in. The only solution for me is Christ's will, and His will is something I receive when I receive Him.

Another significant point with regard to this matter of choice is this: Jesus Himself tells us that we did not choose Him even at the beginning of our Christian walk, but, rather, He chose us (see John 15:16). In other words, He chose and appointed each one of us for a certain work on this earth, and then He drew each of us by His unfailing love in order to drive us to the point of crying out for mercy and deliverance from our sinful selves (see Jeremiah 31:3; John 12:32). In short, He drew us to the point of confession. Of course, He draws everyone in this way, but most, as I'm sure you know, resist the drawing power of His love and cling instead to their sinful lives of autonomy and rebellion.

The important point is this: Your life in the Lord was not initiated by some noble choice to exercise your will in the right direction by searching for or following the truth. Rather, the Bible says that each of us is drawn to the Lord after He chooses us (see Jeremiah 31:3; John 12:32; John 15:16).

If you are sincere in confessing your need to Him, I believe the Lord will bring you to the point in your own experience where you realize it is only by His grace in Christ that you are where you are. Furthermore, I believe He will show you that any decision or resolution on your part that you might presently think was essential was, in reality, only an expression of how blind you were to your deep and continuing need of His mercy and grace.

As a final point, I should mention that the natural culmination of all this discussion of confession and the will is found in Galatians 2:20. Here Paul writes that:

> *I am crucified with Christ:*
> *nevertheless I live; yet not I,*
> *but Christ liveth in me:*
> *and the life which I now live in the flesh*
> *I live by the faith of the Son of God,*
> *who loved me, and gave Himself for me.*
> *(Galatians 2:20)*

In other words, I am dead. The sin in my life killed me (Romans 7:9-11). When I try to do something, then I am merely bringing the old man of sin back to life, and he is surely not going to do deeds of purity and righteousness, but rather deeds of lawlessness and rebellion. I must continually realize that the walk of faith is one in which it is no longer I who live, but Christ who lives within me. And, as always, the way I lay hold of His life is—not by an act of will—but, rather, by a confession of need.

In summary, then, I would say that no one needs a strong will in order to experience the Lord's salvation. On the contrary, one needs merely a broken one—one that will allow the Lord to replace it with His very own.

I am speaking as one who was broken to the point where

he realized he had no willpower at all. This utter brokenness drove me to the point of crying out to the Almighty for mercy and deliverance. It was this same brokenness that ushered me into the victorious way of resting in Christ and in the power of His will.

Now, one might rise up in opposition to this idea and say something like, "I don't think I want to live my life in a continuous state of confession!" In response, I would say that, until this corruptible puts on incorruption, I don't believe there is any alternative. Living one's life in this way is hard on proud, self-seeking flesh, to be sure, for we naturally want to be in control of things. We want to flex our muscles a bit. But the positive side of this continuing state of contrition is this: it allows the Holy Spirit to probe deeper and deeper into our sinful hearts and thus to reveal the underlying causes of our sin. When we are in the mode of mechanically resolving to do right, we effectively prevent Him from doing this. But as we remain in the mode of honest confession, we allow Him to reveal the deeper personal issues that result in our sinful thoughts, feelings and actions. We likewise allow Him to supply His therapeutic grace at this level at which we are in need of healing.

87

Remember: A straightforward confession of weakness will always eventually lead to a flood of peace and strength, and simple honesty before the Lord is all that is needed in order to be driven to this soul-saving and strength-delivering confession.

Remember also: In any difficulty, be broken, not braced; acknowledge weakness, not strength. For when you are weak (in "willpower"), then are you strong (in Christ) (see 2 Corinthians 12:10).

· P R A I S E   T H E   L O R D ·

CHAPTER 12
FELLOWSHIP

Simple honesty will inevitably drive a person to confess (his or her) need of a Saviour, and confession is all we really need to receive (and *retain!*) salvation. I have made this point strongly and repeatedly in previous chapters. Now I would like to focus on the supernatural *result* of this simple honesty: fellowship.

There is a joy in fellowship that is like none other. It has led to some of the happiest times in my life. Fellowship lifts one above the cares of the world, above the clamorings of sinful flesh, above everything the evil one might attempt to place in one's path. Truly, it is this joy of fellowship that will make heaven a place of bliss.

At its very core, Christian fellowship is a spiritual communion and intimacy that is absolutely foreign to the unconverted of the world. A Christian believer who experiences fellowship with the Father, the Son, and other believers in Christ, experiences a type of spiritual association that others simply cannot share. He (or she) has been grafted into the body of Christ by the Lord's Spirit and experiences a sense of belonging that is in direct contrast to the sense of alienation and estrangement that pervades the unconverted world.

I hope you understand, experience, and appreciate this type of belonging in the body of Christ. None of us, as finite, dependent beings, has a basis for wholeness in himself (or herself). Each of us feels the need to be a coherent part of the larger whole. We all feel the need to "fit in," and if this need is not filled on its deepest level by being brought into union with the source of all being through Christ, then we are left feeling estranged and alienated.

Many are driven by this sense of alienation to compromise themselves in search of superficial fulfillment. They seek intimacy in places where it can be found only on a superficial level—such as promiscuous sex and gang activity.

By contrast, Christian fellowship brings a profound sense of belongingness, derived from the spiritual communion and intimacy that Christians share with the Lord and with other believers.

Another important aspect of fellowship is described by the apostle John in these words:

> *But if we walk in the light, as he is in the light,*
> *We have fellowship one with another.*
> *(1 John 1:7)*

The Bible makes it clear here that if we walk in the *light* (as God is in the light), *then* we will enjoy fellowship with one another.

Light, of course, exposes darkness. It exposes sin. And none of this is pleasant to our flesh! Nevertheless, if we allow ourselves to walk in the path of this exposure (through simple honesty), then beautiful things will begin to happen for us, for we will find that the Lord will draw us into the spiritual communion and intimacy I have been describing, and this communion will form the basis for genuine and fulfilling communication and sharing.

Have you ever been in a position where there was nothing but tension and awkwardness between you and another person? If this situation changed, what brought about the change? Was it not a simple measure of old-fashioned honesty that resulted in mutual confession? In other words, was it not a simple "walk in the light"?

I have found that if just one person in such a tension-filled predicament is willing to humble himself (or herself) enough to confess his part in bringing about the unpleasantness, then the other person will often be drawn by the Spirit of the Lord into a similar posture of confession.

If one person simply says something like, "Hey, John—about last night. I acted like a real jerk. I'm sorry," then the other person will almost always drop his (or her) defenses and say something similar. And the end result will be fellowship that forms the basis of communication and sharing.

But if those involved refuse to deal honestly with the Lord and with others (even with themselves), the end result is an *increase* in tension and awkwardness and an *increase* in alienation and estrangement. When individuals refuse to openly and honestly walk in the light of God, they inevitably feel tense, awkward, and "out of touch" with the Lord, with others, and with themselves. This condition is popularly referred to as "denial," and the state of awkwardness and alienation that results can become so intense in families that mental health professionals refer to it as the "elephant in the living room."

Needless to say, this elephant represents the very opposite of fellowship, for it is something that drives people apart. And it will always be present, in one form or another, whenever individuals' pride prevents them from openly acknowledging the truth by walking in the light.

And walking in the light is synonymous with the sort of honesty and confession that is the one condition of salvation and fellowship in the body of Christ.

When speaking about fellowship, we must recognize that one of the greatest frustrations in our Christian walk can come from trying to be honest and forthright (walk in the light) with another person. Such openness will sometimes result only in misunderstanding and alienation. When I have experienced this, it has been most trying. It is as if the more you try to honestly explain a matter, the more you are misunderstood. Your attempt to walk in the light with another person may drive that person away and leave you enshrouded in darkness.

Such a situation may result because the other person is resisting or denying truth, and the problem will persist until the Lord is able to break down the wall of denial. (Of course, you may in the end discover that it was really *you* who was in a state of denial that caused the alienation! I am focusing here on the person who is seeking to expose truth simply because the person who is seeking to repress it is in no condition to benefit from counsel.) If one party in a relationship is resisting truth, all we can do is continue to bring that person before the Lord in prayer. The Lord is, of course, able to point out to us if we are really the ones causing the alienation.

If you do find yourself in a situation where your attempt to walk in the light with another individual is continually rebuffed, I have found that the best course of action is a tactful retreat. Of course, by the time you realize that you should retreat, you may already have been grossly misunderstood. But don't despair. The Lord can use even that situation to His glory by teaching you to lean more fully upon Him, thus causing you to more completely reflect His image.

Such an experience of being misunderstood can leave you feeling awkward and humiliated, but it can also work a change in you like none other, if you will simply regard it as from the Lord, and will submit to it. Do not try to justify yourself. Simply submit to the misunderstanding and move on.

And remember: No one was more misunderstood than our Saviour!

· **PRAISE THE LORD** ·

CHAPTER 13 · THE · "GOOD · FIGHT OF · FAITH"

I have tried to emphasize in this book that there is nothing we have to do in order to secure our salvation except this: (1) Be honest enough with ourselves and with the Almighty to admit that we are sinners, and (2) Cry out to God for healing and restoration in Christ.

I have also tried to emphasize that this formula never changes. That is, we never reach a point where we are "past" this stage; we never reach a point where we are *beyond* confessing our sinfulness and claiming Christ.

Now, the Bible speaks of the "good fight of faith," and many interpret this phrase in such a way that it seems to contradict what I have just written. That is, many say we must *fight* this good fight, and *fighting* it is something we must *do*.

Now I would say this: If what these individuals mean by "fighting the good fight of faith" is that we must put forth some sort of personal effort or exertion in order to lay hold of or to keep salvation in Christ, then I would strongly disagree. I will once again reiterate I believe that all that we must do in order to get or to keep our salvation is merely to admit our need and then to cry out for deliverance in Christ. The only way one will lose this salvation is if he (or she) ceases to think of himself as a suppliant and begins rather to embrace thoughts of godless independence and autonomy. In short, he begins to think, "I don't need God or His mercy, and neither do you. I'm OK, and you're OK. We can all go this thing alone."

Now if what I have stated is true, then what is one to make

of this "good fight of faith"?

I describe it in this way: The "good fight of faith" is a fight that is initiated, nurtured, and sustained *by faith*.[1] In other words, it is *faith's* fight—and faith is a *gift*.

Thus "fighting the good fight of faith" does not amount to our having to expend any sort of personal effort or exertion in order to get or to keep our salvation; on the contrary, it is the natural result of *resting* in Christ and thus receiving the gift of faith from the Lord. I simply cannot emphasize this point strongly enough. I will repeat it: Fighting the good fight of faith is the natural result of resting in Christ and thus receiving the gift of faith from the Lord. It describes what happens when one is inspired mightily by the Spirit of the living God, when one has been "quickened" to take up the whole armor of God and to enter the battlefield against "principalities and powers" by claiming our Lord's victory every step of the way.

Someone might say, "Yes, faith is a gift, and, as such, it is something that I must simply receive—but it comes by hearing, and hearing comes by the Word of God (see Romans 10:17). Therefore, I must spend time in the Word of God if I expect to receive the gift of faith and thus be able to fight the good fight. This is something I must expend effort and exertion to *do*!"

I would say, "Yes and No." That is, I would certainly agree that one's faith grows as he (or she) spends time in the Word and, through this medium, enters into a living fellowship with his Maker—this, I believe, goes without saying. The critical point, however, is this: One does not have to expend effort or exertion in order to do this, for the Lord is faithful to draw any sincere seeker of truth to Himself (see Jeremiah 31:3; John 12:32), and one whom the Lord draws invariably *hungers* for the Word of God. Such individuals would no more deprive their spirits of this heavenly manna than they would deprive their bodies of the earthly. And why should this surprise us? Surely you have had this experience with the Lord at one time or another. What you must realize is that it is the Lord's will that you have it *continuously*.

Now, if you are not having this experience continuously, then simply confess this to the Lord, and then trust Him to draw you. Do not try to correct the matter yourself by forcing yourself to study God's Word (or by forcing yourself to do anything else). That is not what "fighting the good fight" is all about.

Would you feel honored if someone *forced* himself to abide in your presence? Of course not. Why would you thus think that the Lord is honored if you must force yourself to abide in *His* presence? Clearly, He is not.

So, if you are having trouble finding the time or the inclination to engage in those faith-building exercises like prayer and Bible study, then simply acknowledge this before the Lord in the form of an honest confession. Say, "Lord, I do not find joy in studying Your Word, and I simply cannot bring myself to do it. I am thus asking You to instill within me a living hunger for Your most blessed Word—the same hunger that lived within our Lord Jesus. I claim this in His name. Amen."

A good promise to claim before the Lord in this area is the following:

> **He wakeneth morning by morning,**
> **he wakeneth mine ear to hear as the learned.**
> **(Isaiah 50:4)**

Be assured that the Lord *will* awaken you when you claim this promise, and many Christians find that there is no time like the wee hours of the morning to commune with Him. Truly, this is the time when the heavenly manna is falling. (Remember the experience of the Israelites in the wilderness?) These hours will quickly become the best, best hours of the day for you, because they will be those hours that are spent in fellowship with Him who abounds in steadfast love and mercy. Indeed, it is during these hours more than any other that I have truly come to know the Almighty as my Saviour and my Friend. His presence is always sweet and intense during this time, and its lingering effects invariably empower me for the day ahead. Admittedly, some may find another time of day best suited to their schedule and physical constitution, but whatever that time is for you, the Lord will draw you to Him if you trust Him to.

With regard to my own experience, I can say this: When I was recovering from my bout of depression, I had a very tedious job. But the Lord enlivened this entire period of my life (approximately one year) simply by meeting with me every morning of those trying, trying days. It was almost as if all of the tedium throughout the day didn't matter because I always knew that I would be meeting with the King of the universe the very next morning for counsel and direction. Also, the time of fellowship I would spend with Him during the wee hours would invariably cast a halo of light upon even the darkest days. I can truly say it was during this time when appearances seemed the most hopeless that I first began to realize the fullness of Christ's victory in my be-half. Truly, there is nothing He calls us to go through that amounts to any real hardship, for He always carries the full weight if we merely consent to lay it upon His never-failing shoulders.

So, to summarize:

1. The "good fight of faith" is a fight that is initiated, nurtured, and sustained *by faith*. It is not a fight that implies any independent effort or exertion on our part in order to lay hold of or to keep salvation.

2. The faith that provides the resources for this fight is a free gift that we must simply receive from the Lord.

3. Receiving the gift of faith simply amounts to letting the Lord *draw* us into His fellowship. If one does not resist this drawing of the Almighty, then (he or she) will be drawn into the fellowship of the Lord, he will receive

the gift of faith, and he will thus have the resources to "fight the good fight" by claiming total victory in Christ.

· P R A I S E   T H E   L O R D ·

---

1. Though stated differently, Andrew Murray expresses this thought in his updated work, *The Believer's Prayer Life* (Minneapolis: Bethany House, 1983), 31.

CHAPTER 14 · ABIDING·IN·CHRIST

There is simply no other way to continue to receive fresh supplies of grace than to abide in Christ, that is, to peacefully rest in our Saviour's love. In this chapter I will share some lessons I have learned about abiding in Christ.

Our Lord Jesus Himself uses the metaphor of the attachment of a branch to a vine. Thus, it is clear that just as a branch receives all its support, all its nourishment, and all its elevation from the vine, so do we likewise receive all this from Christ.

Now the problem that arises at this point is this: It is quite easy for us to agree that we receive all our strength and status from our identification with Christ and yet be deluded into thinking that we have obtained an *experience* in a certain area of our Christian walk when, in reality, we have merely obtained an *understanding*. In other words, you and I could talk the theological talk about abiding in Christ as well as anyone, but until we have a personal *experience* of the spiritual rest in Him, then our talk avails us nothing. It is but the expression of theoretical head knowledge that has not yet found its way to the heart. And such knowledge is clearly the most dangerous, for it quite naturally leads the believer to assume that he (or she) possesses in his innermost being what he understands so clearly in his mind, when there is actually not the least connection between these two.

The greatest distance in the world is between the head and the heart. I say this because I have found that when I am the *most* talkative about a certain subject, when I seem to understand it so very, very clearly, that is just the time when I am in the greatest need of examining my own walk with the Lord to ensure that I am not seeking to cover some spiritual deficiency in my heart with empty words from my head. (As the Scriptures say, "When words are many, transgression is not lacking"–Proverbs 10:19, RSV.)

So, the first important lesson to be learned about abiding in Christ is this: We must be sure we are *experiencing* this abiding rather than merely *understanding* it.

The best way to be sure you are experiencing rather than just understanding this is to ask yourself if you truly possess the sense of peaceful rest that inevitably comes when one finally casts the full management of oneself to the Good Shepherd's care. This sense of peace and rest is certainly the most powerful aspect of my own experience, and I believe I can safely assure you that if you truly have this rest, then you are genuinely abiding in our Saviour's care. This is so, I believe, because this profound sense of peace and rest is one that the world simply cannot give; rather, it is given only by One who has *overcome* the world (see John 16:33).

Now if you have any doubt about the precise *nature* of this rest, then I believe the best way to convey it to you is to use a metaphor that has frequently been used by others; namely, that of casting one's full weight upon a nice, soft easy chair. Imagine yourself casting your worn and weary body upon a nice, soft easy chair and passively enjoying the rest and relief that result from allowing the supportive structure of the chair below to carry the full weight of your physical frame. For me, this metaphor captures, as none other, the true essence of what it means to abide in Christ, for just as you invariably experience true physical rest and relief from peacefully abiding in the comfort and security of a nice, soft easy chair, so will you likewise experience true *spiritual* rest and relief by peacefully abiding in the comfort and security of our Saviour's love. You will be as one who has cast the full management of his or her life to another, and all the care and anxiety the world seeks to press upon you will roll onto the shoulders of Him who alone is able to bear it.

Now a significant problem that arises when one is attempting to live this life of peaceful abiding is this: Even though this life is indeed one of rest and peace, the passions that are at work in our sinful members are inclined toward not rest and peace but restlessness and warfare. For this reason, a life of peaceful abiding in Christ is rendered almost impossibly difficult to maintain because we, as the born sinners that we are, are naturally inclined toward an agitated and stimulating life that is characterized by *dis*comfort, *in*security, and *un*rest. In short, the waywardness and rebellion of our sinful hearts is continually prompting us toward a departure from the peace and rest that we find only as we rest in the care of our Saviour. It is as if you were attempting to rest in the comfort and security of the easy chair, and one of your arms or legs was continually extending itself and straining to support the weight of your body. Needless to say, you would experience little physical rest and relief in this predicament. So do we likewise experience little *spiritual* rest and relief when our faculties of mind, emotion, and will are ever seeking to wrest control of a situation and bring its spiritual weight upon ourselves.

Surely you have experienced the peace and rest of abiding in Christ's care, and then—horror of horrors—you find yourself, at times, almost helplessly impelled toward straying from Him whom your soul loves. You find yourself flaunting your independence and relishing the sense of personal autonomy. What should you do when this happens to you?

I believe the answer to these questions is revealed in two most powerful texts of Scripture. Here is the first:

> *But of him are ye in Christ Jesus,*
> *who of God is made unto us wisdom, and righteousness,*
> *and sanctification, and redemption.*
> *(1 Corinthians 1:30)*

Do you see what this text is saying?[1] It is saying that it is none other than *God Himself* who has placed us in the bosom of His Son. You and I can thus rest in the wonderful assurance that it is none other than the will of the Father that we be one with our Saviour. And remember: The Corinthian believers whom Paul was addressing in this letter were, by his own description, "babes in Christ" (1 Corinthians 3:1). That is, they were still very weak in the Lord and were thus subject to a variety of carnal temptations (as the rest of the Corinthian letter reveals). Nevertheless, despite their obvious weakness, feebleness, and carnality, Paul asserts in the strongest terms that they are one with Christ and that God Himself is the One who has effected this miraculous union.

So the first part of the answer to "How are we to abide in Christ?" is this: We must realize that it is none other than God Himself who has planted us in the safety and security of His Son.

Now, in order to get the second and final part of the answer, please consider the following:

> *Now He who establishes us with you in Christ . . .*
> *is God.*
> *(2 Corinthians 1:21, NKJV)*

Do you see what *this* text is saying? It is saying that God is not merely the One who has *planted* us in Christ (as if that were not enough!); He is also the One who *establishes* us there. Precious promise! Think of it: God Himself is telling us that *He* is the One who takes the responsibility of sustaining our spiritual life by keeping us abiding in the place of comfort and rest. Do you see the scope of this promise? If you do, then you will understand that you must look to the Almighty in *all* trial and difficulty, and you must claim Him as the divine "Husbandman" whose every effort and concern is to keep you safe and secure in the absolute power of His Son (see John 15:1).

Now I doubt I can adequately convey to you the sense of

security and peace I received when I first realized God Himself had taken this duty from me. I cannot begin to express the deep sense of rest and gratitude that I felt when I finally realized that I could look to my Father in Christ in every difficulty and know He would surely order all things to keep me safely abiding in the comfort and rest of my Saviour.

And He has done this! Praise the Lord—He has done it. Needless to say, I hope you will allow Him to do the same for you, for I know you will find the most blessed sense of peace and rest when you allow yourself to rest in this promise. Do you not see, reader, how this one Scripture alone could change your life in the Lord dramatically if you but cease all your effort and striving toward abiding, and, instead, look to the Almighty One to keep you where He knows you should be? Trust Him to do this work for you. He knows your sinfulness. He knows your peculiarities of temperament. And yet His Word is still as forceful and clear as it could be: He will *establish* you in Christ.

When our Saviour speaks of this work of our Father to establish us in Christ, He, of course, refers to Him as the "Husbandman" (John 15:1). He then goes on to say that the Father, in this role of husbandman, "prunes" the fruitful branches of the vine so they will not stray from the source of their nourishment and support. Now the significant point to remember, I believe, is this: When our Father in Christ "prunes" us so we will bear more fruit to His glory, this in no way implies that we should be bearing any pain as part of this pruning process. On the contrary, we should be bearing *none* of it, for all this must be cast upon our Saviour. This is what it means to abide in the comfort and rest of Him who bore our griefs and carried our sorrows (see Isaiah 53:4). This is what it means to rest in the security and care of Him who gracefully accepted the chastisement that is necessary for our peace (see Isaiah 53:5). I hope you believe me on this point, for if you do not, then I believe you will grossly misinterpret the Father's work in your life. You will be like so many other Christians I have met—those who believe that this pruning process of God necessitates that they nobly bear the pain and chastisement of the Almighty as good soldiers of the cross. Such believers too often grow colder and deader inside, with less and less compassion for the needy, and less and less sweet love for their Saviour and Lord. And why should this be surprising? For such individuals are attempting to do nothing less than that which Christ has already done *for* us, namely, bear the pain and suffering that is necessary for our redemption.

So, when the providence of your merciful Father orders a "pruning" trial in your life, do not disappoint Him by gritting your teeth and preparing to bear the pain that He has already placed upon His Son; rather, bring joy to His heart by casting the full burden of the trial upon Christ. Let it rest fully and completely upon the never-failing shoulders of Him whom God has given to be your burden-bearer. I believe I can assure you (from painful experience!) that this is the *only* way such trials and "prunings" will produce positive results in your Christian walk.

 But what results they *will* produce if you will just admit to your helplessness and cast the full burden of them upon your Saviour! You will begin to experience as never before what Christ has truly borne for you. If you are like me, then you will find yourself standing back in wonder and awe as you witness Him gracefully accepting every burden that you cast upon Him. You will, in short, find yourself peacefully abiding in His comfort and rest, and you will continually send forth praises to God for mercifully driving you to the refuge of His Son by the "pruning" trials and difficulties He has ordered in your life.

I am convinced that if you will but perceive in every trial and difficulty in your life an opportunity to cast the full weight of its discomfort upon Christ, then you will ultimately be brought to the point where you could be burned at the stake for your faith in Christ, and you would be—like so many others who were providentially led to a similar fate—joyfully singing psalms to your

Saviour's glory. In other words, even if you were to find yourself led to this most undesirable of predicaments, you would *still* find it to be no less true that our Almighty Saviour would bear all the pain and discomfort of the trial. You would have come to know (as have many others) that the Lord's grace *is* sufficient for you (see 2 Corinthians 12:9), that you are *more* than conqueror through Him who loved you (see Romans 8:37), and that He is able to do *exceedingly* abundantly above *all* that you ask or *think*! (see Ephesians 3:20). I don't mean to imply here that Christians will never experience any physical or emotional pain, for pain is given to us to warn or teach us. But Christ will bear us through the pain as we learn to cast it upon Him.

So, in summary, I would say that the key to continual growth and fulfillment in the Christian walk is to abide in the comfort and security of the Saviour's peace, and the way to accomplish this abiding is to look to our Father to keep us resting securely in our Saviour's care. And He does this. (He *does* it!)

> *But the God of all grace, who hath called us*
> *unto his eternal glory by Christ Jesus,*
> *after that ye have suffered a while, make you perfect,*
> *stablish, strengthen, settle you.*
> *(1 Peter 5:10)*

103

(Remember: The suffering mentioned in this text refers to that time when one is learning the lessons of faith and trust in the Saviour, for after one has finally *learned* these lessons, then one should surely cast all of his or her pain and burden upon Christ. The Father and the Son *desire* that we do this—amazing!)

· PRAISE THE LORD ·

---

1. I must once again credit Andrew Murray for clarifying my thought on the topic and the texts I discuss in this chapter. I would heartily recommend to everyone the reading of his book, *Abide in Christ*.

CHAPTER 15

JUST·THE·LORD· AND·YOU

There is a truth about the Christian walk that many learn quite quickly, but others seem to take years to fully understand. It is a powerful truth—one that will result in rapid growth if it is believed and heartily embraced. It can be appropriately summarized by the title of this chapter: "Just the Lord and You."

Now what do I mean by "Just the Lord and You"? Simply this: Everything that comes to you in your Christian walk is from the Lord; therefore, there is never any legitimate cause for feelings of resentment, bitterness, murmuring, or complaint. In saying this, we need to recognize that there is also a great power of evil in the world and that it is Satan, not God, who sends temptations and certain trials our way. But God is concerned about these things and allows only those things to come our way which He knows will lead to our growth if we trust in Him.

A few examples would probably be helpful, so I will ask you to please imagine yourself in the following predicaments:

1. You are driving your car on a city street, and another driver suddenly pulls thoughtlessly in front of you, causing you to stop abruptly. He renders no acknowledgment of having done anything wrong and simply drives merrily on his way.

2. You are trying to be helpful and considerate toward a fellow employee at work, and all your efforts are met with rudeness and insensitivity.

3. You are, by the grace of God, doing your best to complete a job that you believe the Lord has inspired you to do, and, upon completion of the job, you find that all your motives and efforts have been misinterpreted.

Needless to say, all these circumstances could easily cause us to feel resentment or indignation. But let me ask you this: What if all this were from the Lord? (I am not implying that He is the One who directed the driver to cut you off or made the co-worker act rudely or caused people to misinterpret you but rather that He has allowed these trials to come into your life.) What if *every bit* of *everything* that reaches you is directly from His hand?

The important point is this: When one finally realizes that everything in one's Christian walk is directly from the hand of God, then lesser instrumentalities (like other persons, places, and things) drop out of the picture. In other words, we are no longer dealing with other persons who happen to be inconsiderate or insensitive, nor are we dealing with circumstances that seem to conspire against us. On the contrary, we are dealing with *only* the Lord, and He is the sovereign and merciful Ruler who is orchestrating all things for our good. Unpleasant events and circumstances must therefore be received as therapeutic agencies that may, at times, be bitter to the flesh but which will always, when received in a spirit of humility and submission, be healing to the soul.

Have you learned to receive everything (*everything!*) as from the Lord, or do you still wrestle with flesh and blood? If you *do* still wrestle with flesh and blood, then I can assure you that you are missing countless lessons of faith and growth every single day. Remember, the Lord is the God of *all* flesh (see Jeremiah 32:27), and He will use persons and circumstances that you would probably least expect to teach you invaluable lessons of faith and trust if you are open to receive them. You must realize, however, that any murmuring or complaining

105

(under *any* circumstance) is, in effect, directed toward Him; thus, you must cease to do this. You must be thankful in *all* circumstances (see 1 Thessalonians 5:18), realizing that each predicament in which you find yourself is orchestrated by the Almighty, and that His one overriding concern is to make you strong in your faith.

The psalms, especially, are filled with statements about how the Lord is our refuge and how we are safe and secure from all that man can do to us when we abide in Him.

> *He who dwells in the shelter of the Most High,*
> *who abides in the shadow of the Almighty,*
> *will say to the Lord,*
> *"My refuge and my fortress;*
> *my God in whom I trust."*
> *(Psalm 91:1, 2, RSV)*

Listen again to the expressions of these two short verses: "the shelter of the Most High," "the shadow of the Almighty," "my refuge," "my fortress"—this type of expression, which is found over and over again in the psalms, implies that he who abides in the Saviour receives only that which has been divinely prepared for him by the Lord.

There is also the well-known statement of inspiration that is found on page 71 of *Thoughts From the Mount of Blessing*:

The Father's presence encircled Christ, and nothing befell Him but that which infinite love permitted for the blessing of the world. Here was His source of comfort, and it is for us. He who is imbued with the Spirit of Christ abides in Christ. The blow that is aimed at him falls upon the Saviour, who surrounds him with His presence. Whatever comes to him comes from Christ. He has no need to resist evil, for Christ is his defense. Nothing can touch him except by our Lord's permission, and "all things" that are permitted "work together for good to them that love God."[1]

I once read a pamphlet entitled "From the Hand of Jesus" that a sister in the church had given to me. It was written by Elder Frank Phillips, and it included the quotation that is written above. Elder Phillips told of how he had shared this quotation at camp meeting one year with a young wife and mother who had confided that her marriage was "falling apart." He further described how she had embraced the truth contained in these statements and how she had come to him again the next year to tell him the results of applying this truth to her life. She explained to him that the year had brought the unexpected death of her and her husband's eleven-month-old baby. She stated that, shortly after this occurrence, she began to experience "the same old resentments, the same old feelings." She then told of how she "rushed into the bedroom" and confessed these murmurings to the Lord. When a sympathizing member of her church arrived shortly after this confession, she describes what occurred:

107

I looked at this nice lady, put my hand up, and said as kindly as I could, "I don't want to appear to be rude or ungrateful for your kindness, but please don't sympathize with me. You see, I gave my life to Jesus a year ago, and I gave my baby's life to Him at the same time. We are in the hands of Jesus. He knows what He is doing; I don't, but I don't have to know because I trust Him. So, please, instead of sympathy, would you kneel with me, and we can thank Jesus for actually working in our lives.

Would that all of us could respond to such incidents with the faith and courage of this sister in the Lord! Anyway, the end result of this woman's transformed life and her godly example in time of adversity was the conversion of both of her husband's parents. They came to her home shortly after her baby's death and said to her,

> Dear, we've been watching you, watching you for a whole year. Something has happened. You're not the same girl you were a year ago. And we've watched you even closer since the little baby died. We've seen no resentment in you. We don't understand it at all, but we want to tell you something. You see, when we were teenagers, we were members of the Seventh-day Adventist Church, but since our marriage, neither one of us has ever been inside of a Seventh-day Adventist church—never. Our son was raised out of the church entirely. But if God can do in you what He has done in you in one year's time, then He can do it in us too. We're going to come back to church.

She goes on to tell how, shortly afterwards both parents were baptized.

"But that's not all!" she says. "After they were baptized, my husband came home one day and said, 'Honey, you're not the girl that I married. If God can do in you what He has done in this past year, if He can do in my parents what He has done in such a short time, then He can do it in me also.'"

She then exults in stating that "One week ago my husband was baptized, a born-again Christian!"

The woman closes her discussion with Elder Phillips by saying,

> Now I understand! In the earth made new I'm going to have my baby, my little girl, my husband, and his parents! I understand now that God works in marvelous

ways His wonders to perform. I just want you to pray with me that I will never forget this lesson—to accept absolutely everything as coming from Jesus and to give God thanks for it."

I hope that you and I will do the same, reader.

· P R A I S E T H E L O R D ·

---

1. Ellen White, *Thoughts from the Mount of Blessings*. (Boise, Idaho: Pacific Press Publishing Assn., 1956) 71.

CONCLUSION

As I conclude this short work on the interior life of the believer, I find myself filled with the hope that you, the reader, have found it to be of benefit in some way. There have been a number of books the Lord has used to help me grow in His grace, and I sincerely hope this will be one that He is likewise able to use to help you to grow. I believe I can honestly say the writing of this book has been a labor of love, and I thank the Lord, as well as you, the reader, for giving me this opportunity to share my experiences.

I have focused on the *inner* life of the believer who is born again in Christ, and because of this focus, it certainly would not surprise me if many were to take issue with this approach and say something like, "Wait a minute. Why do you focus so much on the *experience* of the believer? Our assurance of salvation rests in the finished work of Christ, not in our interior lives."

Now, it is true that our assurance of salvation rests in the finished work of our Saviour; nevertheless, when we simply acknowledge our need of redemption and then cry out to the Almighty for what He has supplied by His grace in Christ, then the end result is an *experience* with Him. There is simply no way around this. Listen again to what our Lord says,

This is life eternal, that they might know thee the only true God, and Jesus Christ, whom thou hast sent.
(John 17:3)

Now I ask you, How can one know the *Person* of God apart from an interpersonal *relationship* with Him (through the merit of Christ, of course)? Clearly, one cannot.

I can assure you that if you do not personally *know* the Lord, if you do not experience personal *communion* with Him on an ongoing basis, then you do not begin to understand what it means to trust Him for your salvation. How can you possibly trust Someone with whom you have no trusting *relationship*? What then would be the basis of your trust? Printed words on the pages of the Bible? Historical evidence? Nothing along these lines will suffice, for the bottom line in truly being able to trust the Lord is this: He must be *REAL* to you. His very life must be something that you experience as a supernatural presence in your life.

When I was following the Lord (so I thought) in my own "strength," I would read promises in His Word like, "My grace is sufficient for you"; thus, in whatever situation I happened to be in, I would say to myself, "Well, His Word says that His grace is sufficient for me, so I guess I'll have to gut it out."

Too many Christians live their lives in this way. They spend so much of their time resisting temptations, resisting the pull of the world, resisting the natural tendency in themselves toward self-glorification—and they believe that they are doing all of this in the Lord's strength and that they are abiding in His will for their lives. Such people have only faint glimpses of the Lord and His mighty power, for when one has a vibrant and growing fellowship with the Father through the finished work and the ongoing mediation of the Son, then he lives *above* the pull of the world. He sees in those things that formerly allured him only darkness and despair, and he is so very, very thankful that the Lord has drawn him out of their deceptive grasp and into the glorious peace and joy of His grace.

A major concern of mine as I conclude this study is the following: Since it is so very difficult to summarize what one believes to be the important aspects of the Christian walk in a solitary book, I fear that much of the message I have endeavored to convey in this work will be misinterpreted. I have not dwelt upon many of the basic tenets of Christian doctrine, for I assume that most Christians are already familiar with these. Needless to say, I believe that all God's people should be spending much time in His Word and should be reading (and *re*reading) such books as *Steps to Christ, Thoughts From the Mount of Blessing, Christ's Object Lessons, The Desire of Ages*—the list goes on and on. I can state unreservedly that I do not believe that anything that I have written in these pages contradicts anything the Lord has imparted to His church through inspired testimony.

A significant guide for me has been my own experience, but I will quickly add that my own experience is one I diligently and consistently monitor in order to ensure that it is in harmony with the experience of the born-again believer as it is depicted in the Scriptures and in the Spirit of Prophecy. I will readily confess that I have little tolerance for professed believers in Christ who speak only in abstract or theological terms, because I used to do this too. I will also confess that I likewise have little tolerance for those who speak always and everywhere of the believer's forensic justification in Christ without speaking also of one's resultant *experience* in the Lord. This type of dialogue represents, in my view, a very one-sided and distorted presentation of Christian realities. The Lord has created and redeemed us so that we may have *fellowship* with Him. This is the true joy of the Christian walk. It is, quite simply, the very substance of personal salvation.

Of course, we are not to make our experience the absolute, for only the Bible is an infallible guide. Nevertheless, the Bible's guidance is infallible only as its teachings are correctly interpreted by the Holy Spirit, and the Holy Spirit cannot correctly interpret the passages of divine revelation unless His presence is an ongoing reality in our lives.

I have written very little about the issue of personal reform.

·CONCLUSION·

I believe there is much need of this in our church, but I have not focused any attention on it because I believe it will come about only as individuals allow themselves to be drawn into a vibrant and fulfilling fellowship with the Father and the Son. I must emphasize, however, that I do strongly believe the time has come when the Lord is drawing His people into a closer and closer walk with Himself, and thus into a lifestyle that is farther and farther away from the self-indulgent and stimulating ways of the world. He has certainly done this for me, and I regard matters such as simple and nonstimulating diet, dress, and personal lifestyle to be indispensable fruits of His salvation in Christ.

Finally, I will state the obvious; namely, that love truly is the "fulfilling of the law" (Romans 13:10). I hope you never allow the devil to blind you to this truth, and I further hope that you understand beyond a shadow of a doubt that as you grow in your fellowship with the Almighty, likewise will you grow in your experience of that which "bears all things, believes all things, hopes all things, endures all things" (1 Corinthians 13:7).

Truly, love never fails—and neither does He whose very essence is love. This book is written in the fervent hope that you will allow yourself to trust your very life with Him whose unfailing love renders Him none other than the "Father of mercies and God of all comfort" (2 Corinthians 1:3).

· P R A I S E   T H E   L O R D ·

APPENDIX·A

Since the law and the keeping of the law has played such a prominent role in Seventh-day Adventist theology through the years, I have included this appendix to further develop the point I addressed in chapter ten: that the law and the keeping of the law should not be the *focus* for the born-again believer in Christ. Some Adventists would probably disagree with this claim, and they would doubtless support their disagreement with a text like the following:

> ***But he who looks into the perfect law of liberty***
> ***and continues in it,***
> ***and is not a forgetful hearer but a doer of the work,***
> ***this one will be blessed in what he does.***
> ***(James 1:25 NKJV)***

Now, on a surface reading, this text would certainly appear to be saying that the law retains a central usefulness for the converted person. In other words, it would appear to be saying that we should all be setting our focus on the law and then resolving in our hearts to continue in its ways. But when we look at the context in which this scripture appears, it seems clearly to be one in which the law functions as a "mirror" to reveal one's true nature (see James 1:23, 24). Now one's true nature is, of course, sinful, so it seems as if the purpose that the law is serving here is to bring an individual to the point of conviction of sin. (This is consistent with what Paul describes as the purpose of the law in Romans 3:20.)

Now the text does, of course, speak of looking into the perfect law of liberty and continuing in it. Here I would respond that it is only our Saviour who has ever truly done this. In other words, it was only Christ who—in and of Himself—was able to look into the law uncondemned, perceive in it the basis of true liberty, and continue to the bitter end in His perfect performance of its precepts. It thus follows that we are able to do all this only as we abide in Him.

Now this is precisely the point where, I believe, many Adventist Christians stumble. They read a text like James 1:25, and they say, "I'm gonna do that." (In this case, the "doing" amounts to setting one's focus on the law and determining to continue in its lawful ways.)

This is, unfortunately, a sure prescription for disaster. The important point is this: The Lord asks only that I be honest before Him (truly, it is only in this way that He can "reason" with me—Isaiah 1:18). Now if I am merely honest, then I will be driven to the point of acknowledging that I cannot "measure up" to any of the moral imperatives of Scripture. That is, I will be driven to the point of acknowledging that I simply cannot do what I know has to be done. I thus confess my need of *Christ*, and I find that all of the "doing" is *done* in Him. The key to victory then becomes simply *abiding* in the One who is victorious. Now the *central* point is this: the condition of abiding in Christ has nothing at all to do with setting one's focus on the law or the keeping of the law. On the contrary, the condition of abiding in Christ is a simple confession of need.

Another way to look at this matter is the following: As sincere Christians, we will all certainly want to walk, even as Christ walked, and this "walking" will certainly demand that we "continue" in the ways of the law, but this "continuing" in the ways of the law is the *fruit* of our salvation, and fruit is not something that is borne while one concentrates on bearing it. On the contrary, fruit is simply the spontaneous result of one who is growing in God's grace. (You may want to review chapter six in this context.)

The significant point I would seek to emphasize in relation to James 1:25 is the same as the *general* point I seek to emphasize throughout this book; namely, that any moral imperative or condition of blessing that is articulated in Scripture (in this case, "looking into the perfect law of liberty and continuing in it") is one that must be regarded as finding its fulfillment *solely* in Christ. Any perspective that strays from this rigid focus is, in my belief, a works-perspective in one way or another. The bottom line, once again, is simply this: If salvation is truly a gift (and, of course, the Bible asserts that it is), then our part should simply amount to being honest enough to confess our need of it.

If one still feels inclined to dispute the perspective I have offered with regard to God's law and its rightful use, then I would point out where the apostle Paul states in Scripture that liberty is to be found—not where the law is—but rather where the Spirit is (see 2 Corinthians 3:17). This is true because it is the Spirit who brings the perfect fulfillment of the law into each of our hearts when we claim Christ's victory by faith. It is vitally important for each of us to remember that it is only through the law's perfect fulfillment in Christ that it becomes the "perfect law of liberty" for us. Indeed, apart from Christ and His abiding in our hearts by faith (which is maintained through a confession of need), it is clear that the law is not a law of liberty at all, but rather a law of *death*, as Paul states in 2 Corinthians 3:6. (In other words, the law is the vehicle that the Lord employs to bring me to the point where I am crucified with Christ. Once this is done, then I can truly say that it is no longer I who live, but Christ who lives within me [see Galatians 2:20.])

The important point is that the law is never the "perfect law of liberty" for any of us apart from its perfect fulfillment in Christ, and its perfect fulfillment in Christ is something I secure for myself by a simple confession of need. I *never* get beyond this point of confessing my need. I *never* get to the point where I can say, "By God's grace I can do such and such (look into the law and continue in it)." Why? Well, because the Bible is clear that God's grace is found only *in Christ*. And the way I lay hold of this is by allowing the "I," so to speak, to drop out of the picture. In other words, the way I lay hold of God's grace in Christ is to confess that I am *totally* in need of Christ's merit (I am not just in need of a little of God's "grace" to empower me to do good things). What I then find is that as I safely abide in Christ, all of the necessary "doing" of the Christian walk gets done as the *fruit* of my salvation and subsequent growth in grace.

· P R A I S E   T H E   L O R D ·

117

APPENDIX·B

I am including this appendix for the purpose of providing a more in-depth analysis of the Spirit of Prophecy statement that "Everything depends upon the right action of the will." I am doing this because I believe that some in our church have misinterpreted and misapplied this statement and have thus promoted a religion that depends upon the power of the will rather than upon simple honesty before the Lord.

Probably the best place to start this discussion is with the little book *Steps to Christ*. In the chapter on consecration, we read the following:

What you need to understand is the true force of the will. This is the governing power in the nature of man, the power of decision, or of choice. Everything depends on the right action of the will. The power of choice God has given to men; it is theirs to exercise. You cannot change your heart, you cannot of yourself give to God its affections; but you can *choose* to serve Him[1] (page 47).

Now, taken by itself, this series of statements would certainly seem to imply that the way to acquire victory in the Christian life is to *choose* to serve God. In other words, it seems to imply that everything hinges upon the right action of our wills and that all of us are thus in the position of having to use this faculty of the will properly if we are ever to be successful in the Christian walk.

But please get out your own copy of *Steps to Christ* and look closely at the context of these statements. In the sentence that precedes the passage I cited, Sister White writes the following: "The knowledge of your broken promises and forfeited pledges weakens your confidence in your own sincerity, and causes you to feel that God cannot accept you" (47). Clearly, someone who has broken so many promises and forfeited so many pledges to God that he is driven to the point of actually doubting his own sincerity is certainly *not* someone who is in a position to *choose* to serve God. Indeed, the very *impossibility* of choosing to serve God has obviously been the problem for such an individual all along. That is, he has *already* promised to serve God, he has *already* resolved to do His will, but, as Sister White states (in another statement that immediately precedes the passage that I cited), his "promises and resolutions are like ropes of sand" (47).

So, it seems clear from the context that the Spirit of Prophecy is clearly *not* stating that the way to serve the Lord is simply to choose to do so. Such a position is, I believe, quite shallow, and it does not even *begin* to take into account the force and the reality of sin in the life of one who is seeking to do God's bidding. As I have stated earlier in this work, if I had thought (when I really hit bottom) that everything in my salvation depended upon the right action of my will, then I would surely have packed it in. Again, the reason is that the very *problem* was with my will.

So, what then *is* the point of these Spirit of Prophecy statements about the will if one cannot, in fact, simply choose to serve God? Well, first of all, look at the opening statement of the paragraph under investigation. It reads, "Many are inquiring, 'How am I to make the surrender of myself to God?'" (47). In answer, we can expect an explanation of *surrender*, and sur-

119

render, by the very meaning of the term, implies an admission of something we *cannot* do, not about something we *can*. Needless to say, since Sister White is writing about surrender, about admitting to what we *cannot* do, then we would expect her statements concerning the will to be related to this theme, and they are.

In order to see the connection between surrender and the will, simply look at the sentence that comes immediately after the series of statements that I initially cited. The last statement in that series is this: "You can choose to serve Him" (47). Now the *very next* statement (which I believe functions as an obvious explanation) is this: "You can give Him your will" (47). Clearly, the act of giving the Lord my will is an act of confession and surrender. In other words, it is an act in which I essentially confess that my will is in bondage to sin, and I subsequently cry out to the Lord and ask that He take possession of it in order that it may be used to will and to work according to His good pleasure.

Now, if you will look at the two paragraphs that come immediately after the paragraph that we have been examining (these are the final two paragraphs in the chapter), you will see that Sister White mentions our need to "choose to be Christians" as well as our need to employ a "right exercise of the will." In each instance, however, she once again explains the meaning of this "choosing" and this "exercise" by equating each with a "yielding" of the will to God. The point, once again, is that she is obviously writing about acts of confession and surrender, not about acts of "willpower."

As a final commentary on this matter of the Spirit of Prophecy and the role of the will in salvation, I will note that Ellen White wrote in her diary in 1891 about those "who speak of religion as a matter of the will. They dwell upon stern duty as if it were a master ruling with a scepter of iron—a master stern, inflexible, all-powerful, devoid of the sweet, melting love and tender compassion of Christ."[2]

Clearly, Ellen White did not believe that religion was "a matter of the will."

1. Ellen G. White. *Steps to Christ* (Boise, Idaho: Pacific Press Publishing Assn., 1956), 47.

2. Ellen G. White Diary, February 27, 1991. Cited in George R. Knight, *From 1888 to Apostasy* (Washington, D.C.: Review and Herald, 1987), 68-69.

APPENDIX·C

About a year or two ago, I felt the Lord was leading me to write a Bible study that was grounded in my own personal testimony of deliverance. I have used this study for quite some time in a prison ministry in which I am involved, and many individuals to whom I have given it have told me that it was very helpful (praise the Lord). I am including it as an appendix in this book since it covers much material in a personal way that is closely related to the topic of one's interior life of righteousness by faith.

A New Life

Do you feel remorse about the way you have lived your life?

Did you once have many hopes and dreams, but now find yourself with only disappointments and regrets?

Do you sometimes feel that God is punishing you?

If you answered Yes to any of the above questions, then you must understand that there is hope for you. God is fully able to reach you with His healing grace and His cleansing power. Furthermore, He *desires* to reach you. He *desires* to give you His peace, His joy, His power, and His love. He *desires* to give you a new life.

It does not matter that you have repeatedly sinned against Him, for He will forgive you.

It does not matter that you are burdened with pain, remorse, and regret, for He will lift you beyond it.

It does not matter that you deserve to be punished, for He has borne the punishment for you.

In the following study, you will learn how to enter into joyful communion with your Saviour and your God. You will also learn how to grow in this relationship and to claim the boundless riches that are yours because of God's great mercy and grace.

Remember: God is fully able and longs to deliver you—regardless of your present circumstances or your past life. Understand this. Sin-sick and burdened souls (like myself) have come to Him over and over again since this world began, and He has always healed and restored them when they approached Him in sincerity and in truth. If you are tired of trying to make it on your own and are willing to let the Almighty begin to work for you, then He can and will give you a new life.

Trust Him to do this for you.
Trust Him! You Can Have a New Life.

A Future and a Hope

123

I remember reading a story that illustrated a very important point. The story told of the day the devil held an auction in order to sell to his demons all the devices he had used to tempt sinful mortals. Almost every device that went up for bidding was shiny and new, and it was apparent these devices had hardly been used by the devil at all. This was true of all the devices except the last one. This last device represented the temptation the devil had found to be the most successful in securing his prey. It was very worn, and it was obvious it had been put to much use. The bidding soared higher and higher as the demons in attendance recognized the value and power of this temptation to lead souls to ruin. At one point a bystander asked what this temptation was. He was told,

"It is the temptation to despair."

Now you must understand, reader, that *all* of the devil's temptations culminate with the temptation to despair. In other words, all his other temptations are merely devices that he employs in order to get you to the point where you believe your case is hopeless. Once he has you believing this, he knows he has you secure in his grasp.

What you must understand, therefore, is that regardless of how sin-sick, polluted, and desperate you know yourself to be, God *longs* to forgive you and to restore you. He *longs* to give you hope. Furthermore, He is fully able to do this, for He has all power at His command.

There is only one thing that you must do: *Trust Him*.

Now you might say, "I could never trust God to deliver me. I have made too much of a mess of my life."

Guess what? I once said that, and God has delivered me! Furthermore, I know many others who once said that, and God has delivered them! Now if God has delivered all of us (and He has), then what makes you think He cannot deliver you?

 Remember: All of us thought *exactly* what you might be thinking. That is, we *all* thought that God could *never* deliver us. We *all* thought that we had made too much of a mess of our lives. But God *did* deliver us—*every one* of us. The lesson each of us learned along the way is this: God is in the business of *restoring* messed-up human lives.

Yes, God is in the business of doing this. He delights to do this. And He will do this for you if you will simply let Him.

Tell me, reader, why would you think that God would not do this for you?

Do you think He has no *power* to do this for you?

Do you think that He does not *want* to do this for you?

Do you think that you are too *sinful* or too *hopeless* or too *depressed* for Him to do this for you?

If you are thinking any of these thoughts, then I can assure you that you are *wrong*.

You might say, "How do you know I am wrong?"

I say, "I know you are wrong because I have finally come to the point in my life where I choose to *Listen to God's Word*, and His Word says, quite clearly, that God desires to *prosper* you, to *restore* you, and to give you *hope*."

Now please understand, reader, that listening to God's Word is the indispensable key that will allow you to know God's thoughts toward you as well as His will for your life. This is what you must begin to do. You must begin to *listen to His Word*.

God speaks to you through His Word.

He communicates His Will for you through His Word.

He enters into joyful communion with you through His Word.

Clearly, then, it is of the utmost importance that you *listen to His Word*.

In the remainder of this lesson, we will be listening to what God's Word says to us about His thoughts toward sinners like you and me. Specifically, we will be listening to what His Word says about His desire to give us a *future* and a *hope*.

You will remember that we began this lesson by noticing that *all* of the devil's temptations culminate with the temptation to despair. What this means is that the devil does everything he can in order to get you and me to the point where we will believe that our cases are hopeless. Never forget that this is the way the devil operates. I will state it once again:

The devil does everything he can in order to get you and me to the point where we will believe that our cases are hopeless.

Now the way that the devil does this is the same for every person. First of all, he leads us on, step by step, in a path of pride and self-sufficiency. In other words, he leads us in a path where we believe that we can make it on our own without God. He doesn't care much what we do in this path; the important concern for him is simply this: he seeks to attract our attention to something in *this* world so we will live our lives without looking to God for guidance and direction.

Now when our own way has resulted in disaster (as it always does—sooner or later), and we have really hit rock-bottom, the devil then presents our sin-sick and polluted lives before us and says, "You are too great a sinner for God to help. Nothing in your life will ever change. Your case is hopeless. You are destined to live a life of misery and then rot in hell."

Once again, I will ask you never to forget that this is the way the devil operates. He works to lead you on, step by step, down a path of ruin until he has you feeling so desperate and so far from God that you believe your case is hopeless. The important point you must understand is this: if you are feeling this sense of hopelessness, then you can be sure that it is from the devil, not from God. I repeat:

A sense of hopelessness is from the devil, not from God.

God always seeks to inspire you with courage and with hope, never with discouragement and despair. Understand this. *God seeks to inspire you with hope.*

Now you might ask, "How can I be sure God wants to inspire me with hope?"

Listen to His Word:

*I know the plans I have for you, says the Lord,
plans for welfare and not for evil,
to give you a future and a hope.
(Jeremiah 29:11, RSV)*

And, again, listen to His Word:

*Beloved, I wish above all things that thou mayest
prosper and be in health,
even as thy soul prospereth.
(3 John 2)*

So this point is settled, right?

Please understand that you cannot say, "Yes, but ... " There are no "buts". The Word of God is just too clear in this area.

He *desires* to prosper you. He *desires* to give you a future and a hope.

We have listened to God's Word, and His Word is very clear. Therefore, the issue is settled.

Now you might say, "But I have lived an awful life, and my sin has separated me from God and from the hope and the prosperity He desires to give me."

It is certainly true that sin separates us from God (see Isaiah 59:2), but what is God's solution to this?

Listen to His Word:

> *If we confess our sins, he is faithful and just*
> *to forgive us our sins,*
> *and to cleanse us from all unrighteousness.*
> *(1 John 1:9)*

Here God promises to be faithful and just to forgive us our sins if we simply confess them to Him.

Once again, listen to His Word:

> *Only acknowledge thine iniquity,*
> *that thou hast transgressed against the Lord thy God.*
> *(Jeremiah 3:13)*

This is all that God asks. Simply humble yourself enough to acknowledge to Him that you have committed iniquity and have transgressed against Him. Then ask for His forgiveness. If you ask this with a contrite heart that is truly sorry for having committed sin (see Psalm 51:17), then His Word says that He is faithful to forgive you. In fact, the Word of God says He will take all your sins and cast them into the depths of the sea (see Micah 7:19).

Once again, we have listened to God's Word, and, once

again, His Word is very clear.

Therefore, the issue is settled.

But you might say, "I know God promises to forgive me, but I have sinned *greatly*, and my heart still condemns me."

Listen to His Word:

> ***If our heart condemn us,***
> ***God is greater than our heart,***
> ***and knoweth all things.***
> ***(1 John 3:20)***

Do you understand what the Word of God is saying here? It is saying God is *greater* than our hearts. This truth should be obvious to all of us, but it is a truth we often lose sight of during those times when the devil accuses our consciences and brings up our past sins before us. The devil knows if he can get us to believe the testimony of our sinful hearts rather than the testimony of God's Word, then he will be able to convince us we are hopeless sinners whom God cannot forgive. The truth, however, is precisely as the Word of God states it. God is *greater* than our hearts, so we must take the testimony of His Word *above* the testimony of our feelings. I repeat,

> **We must take the testimony of God's Word**
> **above the testimony of our feelings.**

I hope you will *never* forget the previous statement, reader, for it will be a safeguarding principle that will keep you settled and secure in your future experience with God. Certainly we all know how easy it is to be swayed by our feelings and to treat them as true indicators of our condition. The truth of the matter, however, is that feelings can be very misleading. This is because our hearts are, as the Word of God says, "deceitful above all things, and desperately wicked" (Jeremiah 17:9). For this reason, we cannot always trust the feelings or the impressions of our sinful and changeable hearts—however forceful or convincing they might seem to be. We *can*, however, always trust the Word of the living God, and this Word says God forgives us when we confess our sins to Him, so you must believe this—regardless of the testimony of your heart.

You should understand that God's Word also says the following,

It is God that justifieth. Who is he that condemneth? (Romans 8:33, 34)

This passage of Scripture is saying that God is Someone who *justifies*; it then goes on to ask, "Who is he that condemns?"

Actually, the Bible *reveals* to us in other passages who it is that condemns. Do you know who it is? It is the devil. The Bible refers to him as the "accuser of the brethren," and it says that he "accuses" us "before our God day and night" (Revelation 12:10). It is important that you understand that all condemnation is from the devil. I repeat,

All condemnation is from the devil.

God *never* condemns. On the contrary, He always *justifies* and *forgives*.

Now if you find that you do not feel justified and forgiven, even after you have confessed your sins to God openly and sincerely, then please understand that this is because the devil has gotten a foothold in your heart because of all the years you allowed him to have his way with you. He is doing all he can to make you feel sinful and condemned, and he is doing this in a last desperate attempt to convince you that you are not forgiven and justified by God. You must realize that this feeling does not affect your status before the Almighty. His Word says that you are forgiven and justified, so you must believe this. (You must *believe* it.)

I can assure you, as one who has been through all this myself, if you will simply persist in believing the testimony of God's Word and in refusing to believe the testimony of your sinful heart, then you will soon be ushered into a rich experience where you will have a glorious sense of your pardon and acceptance with God. This is what you want, right? Understand and believe that this is what God wants as well. And He will bring it to pass if you will simply trust Him and His Word to you.

Once again, the issue is settled.

You might say, "But I believe that God despises me."
Listen to His Word:

> ### *Behold, God is mighty, and does not despise any.*
> ### *(Job 36:5, RSV)*

It is a lie of the devil that causes anyone to believe that God is capable of despising someone. It is the *devil* who is capable of despising. In fact, the devil despises *everyone*. He despises you, and he despises me. He will thus do anything to destroy us. The Bible says he "was a murderer from the beginning, and has nothing to do with the truth, because there is no truth in him." It also says that "when he lies, he speaks according to his own nature, for he is a liar and the father of lies" (John 8:44, RSV).

The devil knows the best lie for him to try to get us to believe is that we are so sinful that God hates us. Never believe this. *Never.* If you find this thought entering your mind at any time, then you can be certain it is not prompted by God. It is a lie of the devil. Always understand this.

It is a lie of the devil.

The Bible is very clear from beginning to end that the essence of God is love (see 1 John 4:8). And since God is an eternal being, is also clear that His love endures forever (see Psalm 107:1). Now, clearly, a being whose very essence is everlasting love is not capable of hating anyone at anytime. On the contrary, a loving Creator like this would love and care for all the beings He has created (as God does), and He would long to save them for His eternal kingdom.

Once again, the issue is settled.

You might say, "But I have done so many terrible things; my life has become like a curse to me."

Listen to His Word:

> **The Lord thy God turned the curse**
> **into a blessing unto thee,**
> **because the Lord thy God loved thee.**
> **(Deuteronomy 23:5)**

You must understand that God is fully able to do this. He has done it for me, and He has done it for countless others as well. He can take the darkest stain in your life and turn it into a blessing that will abound to His glory.

You might say, "No way." But think of this: If you are now in a state of hopelessness and despair because of the sin of your past life, the pollution of your heart, and the unpromising nature of your present circumstances, then imagine how your testimony would inspire hope and courage in others if you would allow God to deliver you from this. Would not this alone turn the curse into a blessing?

Trust Him to fulfill His Word to you.

"But I have wasted so many years," you might say. "My life is over."

Listen to His Word:

> **I will restore to you the years that the locust**
> **hath eaten, . . .**
> **ye shall eat in plenty, and be satisfied,**
> **and praise the name of the Lord your God,**
> **that hath dealt wondrously with you.**
> **(Joel 2:25, 26)**

Do you understand what God is saying to you here? He is saying He will *restore* to you the wasted years you have squandered. Once again, I can truthfully testify that He has done this for me and for many others. He will do it for you.

"How will He do this," you ask?

First of all, He will do it by giving you such peace and joy that you will find yourself lifted *above* all the remorse and regret that now burden you about the shameful and unproductive years of your past.

Second, He will give your life meaning and direction. He will guide you into a fruitful path, and you will find yourself so utterly fulfilled by the sense of purpose that He will give to your life that you will actually find yourself living a brand *new* life. (God *will* do this for you!) It will be as if the wasted years had never happened.

Finally, God will renew your strength. He will restore your youthful vigor. Do you believe He will do this for you? He has done it for me, and I know many others for whom He has done it as well.

Listen to what His unfailing Word says:

> ***Bless the Lord, O my soul,***
> ***and forget not all his benefits:***
> ***Who forgiveth all thine iniquities;***
> ***who healeth all thy diseases;***
> ***Who redeemeth thy life from destruction;***
> ***who crowneth thee with lovingkindness***
> ***and tender mercies;***
> ***Who satisfieth thy mouth with good things;***
> ***So that thy youth is renewed like the eagle's.***
> ***(Psalm 103:2-5)***

And, again, listen to His Word:

> ***Let his flesh become fresh with youth;***
> ***let him return to the days of his youthful vigor.***
> ***(Job 33:25, RSV)***

Now the one thing from your youth that you can be sure God will *not* allow you to retain is the shame. This He will cause you to forget. *(Praise the Lord!)*

Again, listen to His Word:

> **Fear not; for thou shalt not be ashamed:**
> **neither be thou confounded;**
> **for thou shalt not be put to shame:**
> **for thou shalt forget the shame of thy youth.**
> **(Isaiah 54:4)**

Now let me ask you something, reader: Is there any other reason that comes to your mind that causes you to believe God will not or cannot restore you? If there is, then I can assure you that if you will just search the Word of God for yourself, then you will find a promise of the Almighty that reveals to you that your "reason" is not really a reason at all.

I must emphasize that I had reached a point in my life where I had probably a hundred reasons why God could not restore me. I was as hopeless as a hopeless person can get. (Believe me, I was *hopeless*.) But when I began to search the Word of God as for hidden treasure, I found something I thought I could never find, namely,

Hope.

I also found *life*—the very life of God, and this life of God immediately began to renew all the deadness in my soul and inspire me with courage and strength.

I eventually realized that any "reason" I could give as to why God could not restore me—well, God had already thought of it! Furthermore, He had already made provision for it!

Had I sinned? No problem. He *forgives*.

Did my heart condemn me? No problem. He is *greater* than my heart.

Was my life a curse? No problem. He could turn it into a *blessing*.

Had I wasted my best years? No problem. He could *restore* them.

Amazing . . . but True!

It *is* true, reader—every bit of it. And you will find this out for yourself—firsthand—if you will simply allow God to fulfill His Word in you.

We have now come to the point in this study where you must learn a very important lesson. I will ask you to please read the following very carefully, as I must initially develop a few points before I am able to state this lesson explicitly.

First of all, you must realize that all of us end up messing up our lives in one way or another. You must realize also that God is prepared for this. Actually, He was expecting it all along. He did not want it to happen, of course, but there was really nothing He could have done to prevent it without imposing His will upon us, and God will never do this. If we choose to ignore Him and thus do not look to Him for guidance and direction, then He will not force Himself upon us. He lets us walk in the paths of our wayward hearts, and He hopes that—at some point—we will see the futility of trying to find satisfaction and fulfillment apart from Him. It is usually when we reach a crisis that we finally realize this.

"Why does it take a crisis," you ask?

Simply because a crisis is what is usually required to get through to our proud and sinful hearts.

Now when we do reach this point of crisis and we think that our lives are over, God is there to say, "I can fix it."

Understand this, reader. God Himself says,

"I can fix it."

Remember: God knows the end from the beginning, so He

is not taken by surprise when our stubborn and arrogant ways lead us to a "crash." Also, He has all resources at His command. He could bring a hundred different persons, places, or things into your life right now of which you know nothing, and any one of these could change your life completely.

Now how do I know that God can fix even your life? Listen to His Word:

> *I have loved you with an everlasting love;*
> *I have drawn you with loving-kindness.*
> *I will build you up again*
> *and you will be rebuilt, . . .*
> *Again you will take up your tambourines*
> *and go out to dance with the joyful.*
> *(Jeremiah 31:3, 4, NIV)*

I hope you will not respond to that passage of Scripture the way I did when I was in my state of hopelessness. I remember that my sister wrote it on the front page of a Bible she gave to me, and she emphasized how this was God's promise to me. I recall saying to myself, "No way."

I could write a lot about how hopeless and depressed I was at this time, but the point I wish to make is this: God fulfilled this promise to me in spite of my initial unbelief. I see now that He did this in answer to the prayers of many others in my behalf. And guess what? I am praying for you! (I pray for everyone who reads this study!) And guess what again? I know many others who are praying for you as well! (I have asked them to pray for those who read this study!) So I know God will answer our prayers in your behalf in the same way He answered others' prayers in my behalf.

The end result of all this is that God will answer our prayers and fulfill His Word to you if you simply do not resist His working in your life. He will draw you with His lovingkindness (as He did with me). He will build you up again (as He did with me). And you will find yourself going out one day to "dance with the joyful" (as I do—though I once thought this would never be possible).

We have now covered everything necessary in order for you to learn the important lesson of this study. Are you ready for it? Here it is: If you believe you have messed up your life in one way or another (or possibly in all ways), then you can choose one of two options, and the choice you make will determine the entire direction and destiny of the rest of your life. I will repeat this statement because I believe it is of utmost importance:

> *If you believe you have messed up your life*
> *in one way or another (or possibly in all ways),*
> *then you can choose one of two options,*
> *and the choice you make will determine the entire*
> *direction and destiny of the rest of your life.*

Now your options are these:

You can moan and groan and gripe and complain about all the stupid and boneheaded things you have done in your life, or you can

Trust God.

Do you see clearly that these are your two options?

Please understand, reader, that the issue is no longer that you have messed up your life, because Someone has pledged Himself to fix it for you. Furthermore, this Person who has pledged Himself to fix it for you is none other than . . . God!

The only issue now, therefore, is this:

Will you admit that you need help, and will you let God help you?

I will state once again that the issue is *not* that you have messed up your life, because God Himself has pledged to fix it for you. You must merely trust Him enough to let Him have His way in your life without resisting Him.

Now let me tell you something, reader: If you will trust God and not resist Him, then you will have a new life (a *new life*). It is that simple. God will rebuild and restore you completely, and, as I have already stated, you will one day find yourself going out to "dance with the joyful." This may seem impossible to you (as it once seemed impossible to me), but you must remember that "with God nothing shall be impossible" *(Luke 1:37)*.

Now let me tell you one more thing: If you will not trust God and you choose rather to resist His almighty love and power, then you will retain your old, messed-up life, and you will be destined to moan and complain for the rest of your days.

So, what will you do?

Will you trust God? Will you let Him give you a new life? This is the issue, friend. This is the only issue.

You must *trust* the God who created you.
You must *let* Him fulfill His Word to you.
Remember,

Trust and don't resist.

Or, as many say,

137

Let go and let God.

As you think about the many promises of God we have studied in this lesson, please understand that you must begin to claim these promises as if they were made to you personally (because they were). You must not think of them as promises God is making to someone else. Rather, you must think of them as promises He is making to you (because He is). Please understand this. Every promise that we read is a promise God is making to you.

And always remember that God has fulfilled every one of these promises in my life and in the lives of many others. Not one of us was more worthy than you are, yet God fulfilled His Word to each of us. Trust that He will do this for you as well.

As you meditate on these promises and on the great love and mercy of God, you will begin to sense a new creative power working in you. This power is nothing less than the uncreated life of God, and the Bible refers to this life in you as the "Holy Spirit." The Bible also makes it clear that this life in you is that of a Person. Now if you will allow Him, this Person of the Holy Spirit will overrule every other influence that now holds you in bondage, and He will become the governing force in your life. To be "quickened" (as the Bible says) by the Holy Spirit is to live a life that is free from the enslavement of fear and lust. It is a life of joyful communion with God in which one enjoys security and peace "without dread of evil" (Proverbs 1:33, RSV).

There are many important lessons of faith that you will have to learn before your joy in God is made full, and I will warn you now that you will probably stumble and fall many times as you are learning these lessons. Furthermore, there will almost certainly be times when you will become battered and bruised. I tell you this beforehand so you will not become discouraged when you encounter difficult times. Always remember that whoever sets out to trust the Lord fully will encounter trials. They are simply a part of the growing process. Just be sure to understand that God will be with you through every one of the trying times that lie ahead.

As His Word says,

> **Be strong and of good courage;**
> **be not frightened, neither be dismayed;**
> **for the Lord your God is with you wherever you go.**
> **(Joshua 1:9, RSV)**

Trust Him to be with you always, because His Word says that He is. And never forget that God's great purpose in your life from this time forward is to make you strong in your faith and trust in Him. And He will surely do this if you let Him.

Truly, you will come forth as gold.

To summarize this lesson study, then, I will once again emphasize that God does have plans to prosper you. He does desire to give you a future and a hope. He does desire to forgive you and to restore you.

It does not matter that you have sinned against Him.

It does not matter that your heart condemns you.

It does not matter that your life has become a curse to you.

It does not matter that you have wasted what you consider to be the best years of your life.

It Just Does Not Matter.

God still desires to prosper you. He still desires to give you a future and a hope.

And He will . . . if you simply trust Him.

> *Behold, I am the Lord, the God of all flesh;*
> *is anything too hard for me?*
> *(Jeremiah 32:27, RSV)*

You Can Have a New Life.

Where Do You Go From Here?

You may, at this point, be asking yourself questions like the following:

1. "How do I get this new life?"
2. "How will God make it happen?"
3. "Where and when will He begin?"

1. With regard to the first question, the answer is this: You get a new life by simply receiving the promises of God. You will soon discover this is equivalent to receiving His Son, the Lord Jesus Christ.

2. With regard to the second question, the answer is this: God will make it happen one step at a time, and as you take

each step in the path He opens before you, He will reveal more and still more of His glorious plan for your life. You must trust Him in this area. You must trust His promises to you and thus believe He has your best interest at heart and will work "exceeding abundantly above all that we ask or think" (Ephesians 3:20). Do what He gives you the strength to do today, and the tomorrows will begin to look brighter and brighter.

3. With regard to the third question, the answer is this: God will begin here and now. That is, He will start to work with you right where you are, and He will begin just as soon as you cry out to Him for deliverance and guidance. Once again, you must trust Him. Also, you must receive everything in your daily pathway as coming directly from His hand. You must receive it without murmuring and without complaining. He will supply the strength for you to do this, and you will begin to experience a greater and still greater sense of His peace and rest as you surrender to the ordering of His providences and receive everything cheerfully from His hand. You are the clay in the hands of the all-knowing and all-loving Potter. Abandon yourself to His almighty working, and you will not be disappointed. He will bring you forth as conqueror.

Other important points are these:

1. You must begin to spend time with God in Bible study and prayer—especially during the early morning hours. Spending time with the Almighty during this time each day will result in your being drawn into a deep and fulfilling relationship with Him, and this relationship will brace you to meet the various activities of each day with stability and strength.

2. You must get to know God's Son, the Lord Jesus Christ, and you must get to know Him personally. In other words, you must get to know the Lord Jesus as the Person that He is. Ask God to draw you into a strong personal relationship with Jesus as you spend time praying and reading about our Lord's life in the Gospels (Matthew, Mark, Luke, and John). You will soon know the mighty Lord Jesus as your Saviour and your Friend.

3. You must begin fellowshiping with other godly men and women who believe in the Lord Jesus Christ as their Saviour and Lord and who study His Word on a regular basis. Ask God to guide you in this area. You can trust Him to lead you to just the right fellowship that will help make you strong in His strength.

4. You will probably find it helpful to read good Christian books that were written by individuals who have spent much time growing close to the Lord. You will learn many invaluable lessons from these people, and these lessons will probably help you immensely in your walk with God. Again, ask the Lord to guide you in this area.

Some books I would highly recommend are the following:

A. *The Christian's Secret of a Happy Life* (original edition) by Hannah Smith

B. *Steps to Christ* and *The Desire of Ages* by Ellen White

C. *Abide in Christ* by Andrew Murray

5. Finally, you must always remember to *Trust God*. Though your sinful heart will suggest a hundred reasons why He cannot or will not help you—still, you must trust Him. This alone—trust in the almighty and saving power of God—will see you through every circumstance and every difficulty.

Feel free to write at any time.

Stuart Cedrone
P.O. Box 1557
Alvarado, TX 76009

How can one Bible passage possibly Change a person's life Forever?

What happens when a person stumbles upon that "moment of truth" when the written Word becomes the life-changing living Word? Can the Bible possibly pack so much power that its words can transform darkness into light, nonbelievers into believers? Powerful Passages recounts the incredible and inspirational true stories of remarkable Christians throughout history whose pivotal moments in life were their direct encounters with specific Bible passages. After reading each story, you'll want to share them with others. Use them to enhance family worships, provide topics of discussion for prayer groups, or share with shut-ins to brighten their day.

Catalog Number 0164240
ISBN # 0-8163-1337-7
192 pages, paper
US$10.99/Cdn$15.99
  (prices subject to change)